Walking Toward the Light

A journey in forgiveness and death

by Karen Todd Scarpulla

Little White Dog Press

This book is a memoir: The author has made every attempt to recreate events, locales and conversations from her memories of them. In order to maintain their anonymity, the author may have changed or may have left out the names of individuals, places and identifying characteristics and details such as physical properties, occupations and places of residence.

This book is not intended as a substitute for the medical advice of a physician. The reader should regularly consult a physician in matters relating to his/her health and particularly with respect to any symptoms that may require diagnosis or medical attention.

PUBLISHED BY LITTLE WHITE DOG PRESS

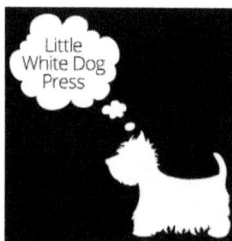

ISBN-10: 0-9891589-1-8
ISBN-13: 978-0-9891589-1-6

First Edition

This book is dedicated to the bravest people I know, my son James and my daughter Kate, who agreed to take this journey with me.

Thank you for allowing me to share our story. You inspire me everyday to reach for the stars.

INTRODUCTION

In 2005, my husband of 16 years and I divorced for many of the same reasons most couples do. Our divorce was less than amicable, and we had a very rocky relationship in the years after.

Seven years later, I made the bold decision to move my children and myself back in with my ex-husband. Why? He'd just been diagnosed with Stage IV esophageal cancer. His life would be cut short, and his kids would have only a few precious months left with him.

This book is a month-by-month chronicle of our journey through cancer, death and forgiveness. Each month explores a new challenge and all of the decisions we faced as a family struggling with a loved one dying. We were unprepared for the sacrifices and difficulties inherent in allowing a family member to die at home.

Through journal entries, I share the emotions I experienced amidst making the heart-wrenching decision to focus on his quality of life versus his quantity of life. We all live with the fear of death, but it is a natural part of life's process. My children and I experienced firsthand the grace that happens when you let go of that fear.

I share with you my path to forgiveness. I provide you with the framework that I used to create forgiveness and truly live it on a daily basis. I had often heard how powerful forgiveness is, but I had so many emotional scars that I didn't think it possible. When I consciously focused on creating a plan to forgive and carried it through, I felt empowered and filled with grace. Forgiving is not easy, but the rewards are worth the journey.

This is my story... It began November 15th, 2011.

CHAPTER ONE

NOVEMBER — SYNCHRONICITY

I am driving home at the end of a very long day at the office. The night is dark and cold, and I cannot wait to get home and take a long and much-deserved hot bath.

Almost four years ago, I launched a marketing company, and this year, I have taken on a business partner. We have decided to expand the business from marketing and sales development to include training workshops for small business owners, as well. The task has been daunting. We've developed the curriculum, marketing plan and, ultimately, a sales funnel. We have taken on office space and increased the overhead needed to run the company. While I really enjoy the flexibility of owning a business, I am constantly worried about growing it and maintaining revenue flow. I am preoccupied with thoughts of upcoming meetings when suddenly my phone rings.

It's Vince, my ex-husband.

I grip the steering wheel and ask myself if I am up for one of his calls. We divorced six years ago, but I still have anxiety when we speak. He usually rages at me about some injustice that has happened to him, how life is not going his way or how God is punishing him. On the third ring, I contemplate just letting the call roll to voicemail. Instead, I take a deep breath and answer.

"Hi, Vince!"

Maybe my chipper attitude will help set the tone for a positive exchange.

"Karen, I just wanted to call and let you know that I just left my endoscopy, and it's not good news," he says. "I have cancer."

Cancer.

The word takes my breath away. I am paralyzed and cannot speak. I then remember that Vince can often be melodramatic for my benefit. He has called me many times in the past to spout off about health issues. Eventually, they all turned out to be very minor problems. I take a deep breath again and reassure myself that this is one of those times.

I can barely hear Vince as he begins to talk.

"It's bad, Karen. The doctor told me that he doesn't know how I have been eating. I have a tumor that is taking up 75% of my esophagus and another tumor in my stomach taking up 50%."

I feel like I am going to be sick. I look up at the road and wonder how I am still driving. *Maybe I should pull over?*

"He said they are the largest tumors he has ever seen. He took biopsies and is sending the pathology to my primary doctor. It's not good, Karen."

"I'm sorry. I'm so sorry, Vince. I don't know what to say except, I am sorry."

"I've already told James," Vince says.

Immediately, I am reengaged. *Why did he tell James?* Wouldn't it be better to wait until he has more information? James must be so scared. During times of stress, Vince often leans on the kids for emotional support as if they are adults. I can only imagine the conversation he had with James.

"I will tell Kate when I see her next," Vince adds.

"Vince, I am so very sorry. We'll get through this."

***

I pull into the driveway and run into the house to the nearest bathroom. Life has just kicked me in the stomach. I can feel my lunch turning, and suddenly it explodes out of my body.

My phone rings again. I am numb. I don't want to answer, but it is my real estate agent, and she rarely calls unless she needs something.

"Hello?"

"Hi, Karen. I have some good news for you. The couple who was in twice to look at your house is bringing in an offer tonight. I will send it over via email as soon as I have it ready."

"That's great news." My voice is completely flat.

"Is everything okay?" she asks.

"Yes, everything is great. Long day. That's really great news. Talk to you tomorrow."

I hang up.

Kate, my daughter, has wandered into the kitchen.

"What's going on?"

"We just got an offer on the house."

"That's good, right?"

"Yes, of course."

"Have you talked to Dad?"

"Yes, I did briefly."

"I tried to call him, but he didn't pick up," Kate says. "I want to know how his appointment went."

Vince had shared with the children that he was having an endoscopy to rule out cancer. I had initially assured Kate she shouldn't worry and that the test was just a precaution. He would be fine. He probably just had a really bad case of acid reflux. How wrong I was.

My phone rings yet again. This time it's James.

"Hi, Buddy," I say.

"I talked to Dad. He says he has cancer."

"Yes."

I choose my words carefully, because Kate is standing nearby.

"So, you know?" he asks.

"Yes. How are you?"

"I'm fine. I don't think it's as bad as he thinks. He hasn't even seen the doctor yet."

"You're right," I say.

But deep down, I am concerned and worried it really is a big deal. Kate asks to speak with James, so I put her on the phone.

"Have you talked to Dad?" Kate asks. "What did he say?"

Kate gets frustrated and shoves the phone back at me.

"What the hell?" James says. "Why did you put her on the phone? You really put me on the spot. Thanks a lot."

He is absolutely right.

"I'm sorry."

What am I thinking putting Kate on the phone? I have to pull myself together, and, more importantly, I need to consider my actions carefully. I don't want to alarm or upset the kids anymore than necessary. James is right. We do not have enough news yet to really worry.

"I'll call you later," he says.

Kate runs by me with her car keys in hand. "I'm going to Dad's house," she calls over her shoulder.

"Wait. I'll drive you."

I can't imagine how upset she will be once she hears the news, and I don't want her behind the wheel of a car. She has only had her license for a few weeks.

Before I can get to the door, she is gone.

I call Vince to let him know Kate is on her way.

"I know," he says. "She just called me."

"Does she know?"

"No. I want to tell her in person."

"She should not drive home alone after you speak to her. Please call me, and I will pick her up."

"I can drive her home. She can pick her car up later."

"Okay. Thank you. And Vince, please know how sorry I am."

"Thanks."

I hang up the phone and have a very strong feeling that all will not be well, and Vince could die. My grief for James and Kate overcomes me.

James is 18 years old and Kate is 16. Neither of them has had a very close relationship with Vince. He has never been a hands-on father. During our marriage, he was away from the family, traveling Monday through Friday for work. The births of both of our children were completely planned, and Vince enjoyed the title of father; however, he never settled into the role. Even when Vince was home with us, he remained distant. He spent his time relaxing, reading the paper, working out and watching sports.

After the divorce, the distance between father and son and father and daughter continued to grow. Vince requested visitation every other weekend. He was supposed to pick the kids up Friday night and return them Sunday evening. However, he usually cut his visits short, either for social reasons or for his work travel schedule. Often the weekend would simply end early because there had been some "Vince" catastrophe—like he had spilled a cup of coffee on the carpet, or he had put a bill in backwards in its corresponding mailing envelope.

Vince sees himself as the victim in everything, especially our divorce, because I'm the one who made the decision. During the process, Vince used the children as his emotional crutch. They were only 10 and 8 at the time and not old enough to fully understand.

As the same-sex parent, I was able to build a relationship with Kate; however, James' same sex parent was absent in his life. I pleaded with Vince to take a more active role with the kids and to consider their feelings during their weekend visits.

At one point, I forced all three of them to see a family counselor, hoping an unbiased, outside party might reach Vince. The children were understandably upset by our divorce. They needed Vince to be the adult and support them emotionally. Unfortunately, the counseling lasted just two sessions before the kids refused to attend. Their reason was very clear. Vince did not listen to the therapist. Each time the children shared their emotions about a particular situation, Vince would come at them with something they had done

5

wrong. It became an episode of the blame game, and this left the children feeling even more vulnerable and isolated when they were with him.

As James matured, his relationship with his father completely deteriorated. Vince saw his own flaws in James and couldn't bear to witness them. Instead of understanding that James was just modeling behavior he had learned from his father, Vince attacked him emotionally. By the time James entered high school, he barely spoke to Vince. And when they did speak, their conversations centered solely on sports, a safe subject.

Of course, the children's relationships with Vince impacted my relationship with each of them. I became an overindulgent parent trying to make up for their feelings of abandonment. James was angry during high school, and I don't think we had a single conversation during those years that did not end in an argument. James spent the last two years of high school at a boarding school. He was much happier living in a supportive environment with plenty of adult mentors.

Now back from boarding school, James lives with Vince. He prefers that arrangement to living with me, because he does not have to abide by any rules.

Kate lives with me. We have a strong relationship, but it's not without its troubles. While I was growing a career, both she and James felt abandoned. I went back to work just six months after the divorce. Up until then, I was a stay-at-home mom. Fortunately, I was offered a job with a marketing agency covering a very large account. On the Thursday I received my offer, I was told I would need to be on a plane Monday to New York for meetings with the clients and their agency. I scrambled over the weekend to hire the first of a string of nannies who would care for the children several days a week. I tried to minimize the impact of my going back to work by working from home two out of five days. Both kids hated this time in their lives. I was traveling and trying to rebuild a career after a 12-year absence. We tried many nannies and never really found the perfect fit. Two years after the divorce, I launched my own marketing agency and began mostly working from home. This allowed me more flexibility. However, by then, James and I were totally at odds, and he barely saw Vince.

***

I pace the floor, fold clothes, wash dishes and pace the floor some more.

A couple of hours go by, and I finally hear the garage door open. Vince must be dropping her off. I run to the door and open it to see her pulling into the garage. *Damn! How could he let her drive home alone?*

"Are you okay?" I ask. Nothing prepares you for talking to your kids about their father's cancer. If only there were guidebooks so I would know how to react and what to say.

"I'm going across the street," she says. "I just want to be with my friends right now."

"Okay. Are you sure?"

I am wounded. She obviously does not feel close enough to me to share her pain. But I quickly realize that this is not about me. This is about James and Kate and how they will navigate their feelings about Vince's illness.

I give her a hug. "Okay. I will see you when you get home."

I walk back inside and dissolve into tears. I'm not even sure why I am crying, but the tears flow and flow. The memories of us being a family and of the early years rush through my mind. I am surprised to feel my heart fill with empathy for Vince.

***

I jump on the treadmill for 30 minutes of walking and 30 minutes of running. This workout is part of my daily routine, but as I hit start on the console and find the belt moving beneath me, my world feels completely different.

I could not sleep the night before. I kept wondering how Vince will get through chemo and radiation treatments and manage to take care of himself. My head swims with questions. How will he feed himself? Who will drive him to chemo? Who will take care of him when he is too sick to get out of bed?

I know he will naturally rely on Kate. Since our divorce, Vince depends on Kate for emotional support. He confides in her as if she were an adult friend. I am very concerned that he will expect Kate to drop everything and take care of him. She is in her junior year, one of the most important as she prepares for college. I envision Kate running back and forth between our houses caring for Vince and studying at home.

The thought makes me amp up the speed for my run. I feel the anxiety present in each stride.

I know Vince very well, and he will need someone to care for him. If there is no one in Chicago to assume this role, he will move back east to live with his mother so she can help. I worry that if he goes to Philadelphia, the children will never see him.

Suddenly, I feel as if the curtains have been pulled back to reveal the answer. I know what needs to be done: Kate and I will move in with Vince and James.

It's not a coincidence that I'm about to receive an offer on the house after it's been on the market for three years. The universe has a funny way of working things out. If I provide support to Vince, then maybe he will stay in Chicago. The children can spend quality time with him and rebuild their relationship. I know deep in my heart that this is the "right thing" to do. I have faith that this will be a turning point for Vince. That he will embrace spending time with the children.

Despite my resolve, I am worried. I worked so hard to divorce Vince, and it was such a scary process. Why would I choose to live with him again?

I slow my pace to a walk, grab my cell and call my mother to tell her everything.

"Why don't you just have Vince and James move in with you at your house?" she suggests.

"Great idea," I tell her, "except I'm pretty sure the house is going to sell. Who knows when I will get another offer?"

I had decided three years earlier to put the house on the market. Between boarding school tuition and the monthly cost to maintain the house, I was drowning financially. I had allowed the kids to stay in their house as long as I could. It was time to sell; however, the housing market had taken a steep dive. There was a surplus of houses on the market in our price range and hardly any buyers.

When my mother and I hang up, I feel even more resolve. My mother supports my decision and understands my desire to have the children mend their relationship with Vince.

Vince has recently been laid off from his job, so he is home all the time now. This will be an excellent opportunity for him to be a hands-on father. I am working long hours and traveling, so he will have quality time with just the kids.

I call my best friend. She doesn't even question me.

"I would expect nothing less of you," she says.

We talk out the logistics for a bit and then say goodbye. I am relieved that two people have confirmed that I am not absolutely crazy.

Next, I call Vince.

"Hi. Vince. How are you doing?"

"Not great. I'm having trouble swallowing and I can't eat or drink first thing in the morning."

"I'm sorry," I say. "Hey, I have meetings downtown this morning but was wondering if I could stop by in the afternoon on my way home to talk to you about something?"

***

It's a sunny day and the drive out of the city is quick and uneventful. I take this as a positive sign from the universe that I am moving in the right direction. I call a few more friends from the car and run my crazy idea by them. Everyone agrees, and they are not surprised at my gesture.

I'm sure Vince is dreading my visit.

Frankly, we dislike each other a lot. Ironically, during our marriage we never argued. Vince would often rage, yell, scream or throw a tantrum, but I very rarely responded. Any response would only escalate the situation, so I became desensitized to his wrath.

Vince and I were married in June of 1988. I was just 23 years old at the time, and Vince had just turned 30. We had been married for 16 years at the time of our divorce. It was a contentious and very scary time for me as I negotiated myself out of my marriage. Vince pleaded and threatened. He was incredulous that I wanted to leave.

Our dysfunctional relationship set up a dangerous parenting dynamic. Vince would be very punitive with the kids, especially James. I would try to make up for his negative parenting style with overly permissive parenting. Neither style is healthy for teenage children. We had both created a real mess over the years.

Now, our anger with each other no longer mattered to me. I love my children more than anything else and I am willing to sacrifice anything for them. I am committed to helping them make peace with their father before it is too late.

If Vince becomes really sick and dies, it will be even more important for James and Kate to mend their relationships with him. I don't want them to have to go through years of therapy because they had unfinished business or left anything unsaid. I know this is what we need to do as a family to heal.

I pull into Vince's driveway and approach the kitchen door. He is sitting in the living room with the TV on. He turns it off as I enter, and I take a seat in a chair directly across from him.

He tells me that he has spent the day calling family and friends to share the news with them.

This is Vince's style. He creates a catastrophe before we know all the facts.

I shift awkwardly in the chair. My throat is dry as I begin to speak. "So I have a crazy idea," I say. "I just heard last night that I will be receiving an offer on my house this week."

"You're kidding. That's great news. Congratulations. You must be really relieved."

"Yes I am. So, my crazy idea is that Kate and I should move in with you and James. This way we can live as a family while you battle cancer."

Vince is visibly stunned. I wait for a reaction.

A single tear streams down his cheek. When he speaks, his voice cracks. "You would do that?"

"I'm convinced that getting an offer on my house is not a coincidence," I say. "It's synchronicity, divine intervention. Think about it. Who will take care of you while you are sick? And this is a great opportunity for you to spend quality time with the kids before they go off to college."

We both sit silently for a long while.

"I don't know what to say."

I immediately feel the need to fill the silence. "So when is your doctor's appointment to hear the pathology report?"

"Friday afternoon."

"Do you want me to come with you? You should have someone there to hear what the doctor has to say."

"That would be great."

I can see he is visibly relieved.

"Let's talk to the kids about moving in and your diagnosis after we see your doctor in a couple of days."

"Sounds like a good plan."

There is an awkward moment as I rise to leave. Vince stands, and I think he may try to hug me. Although our meeting has gone well, I'm not ready for that kind of intimacy.

I pat his arm. "Everything will be okay. We will get through this as a family."

***

Vince picks me up on a Friday to meet with his primary physician who is also my doctor. We expect to be ushered into his office, but instead, we are sent to an examination room. Vince sits on the exam table, and I take the only chair. I think that at any moment the doctor will tell the nurse she has made a mistake and move us to his office.

The past few days have flown by. I've been busy with work and consumed with thoughts about negotiating the sale of my home. Usually a move brings excitement, but in this case, I will be moving in with my ex-husband.

I am resolved in my decision to live with Vince, but I am feeling apprehensive. I am worried that I won't be able to keep my feelings contained and that memories from the past will eat away at the present tasks at hand.

The doctor enters. He looks uncomfortable.

"So," he says, "I have received the pathology on your biopsies. Unfortunately, I wish I had better news. You have Stage IV adenoma carcinoma cancer."

My mouth drops open. I had done a little research online regarding types of esophageal cancer and stages. He has the most aggressive type of cancer, and Stage IV is the end.

Vince looks at me and sees my reaction. I quickly close my mouth, grab my phone and begin taking notes.

Vince asks the doctor if we can conference in his cousin, who is also a physician. Once on speakerphone, Vince's cousin asks a string of questions.

"What is the recommended course of treatment at this point?"

Our primary physician suggests that we contact an oncologist immediately, but that any treatment would be palliative.

"So treatment will be palliative versus curative?" Vince's cousin asks.

"Yes."

Vince looks confused. "What does palliative care mean?" he asks.

Vince's physician, who had been leaning on the counter, stands up and takes a deep breath. He exhales slowly. "That means we will keep you as comfortable as possible until the end."

His words strip the color from Vince's face. Vince looks at me with pleading eyes. I can't speak.

"I am sorry to give you this news," the doctor says. "The nurse will be back to draw some blood and check your levels."

He leaves us sitting in silence. I cannot look at Vince. I am ashamed that I don't know what to say. I have always been the fixer in our relationship, and this is something I can't fix. I know that anything I say now will sound completely inadequate.

"Karen?" Vince breaks the silence first. "Did he say I am going to die?"

I turn in my chair and look up at him through tears. "Yes."

Vince begins to cry, too.

The nurse arrives to draw blood.

At some point, we leave the doctor's office. We are silent as we walk to the car.

My phone rings.

It is my real estate agent.

"Hi, Karen. Great news, I finally have the offer. It's a good offer, close to your asking price."

"That's great."

"There is one thing that we may need to discuss."

"What's that?"

They are looking for a 30-day close."

"What! Are you kidding me? That means I would have to move out before Christmas?"

"Yes. I'm sorry."

"No! No! And no! Absolutely no way. Who asks a family to move out right before the holidays?"

Vince listens to my end of the conversation. He reaches over and puts his hand on my arm. "You have somewhere to go. Just say, 'yes.' You don't want to lose the offer."

I take a deep breath.

"Send it over. I will make it work."

Vince and I drive home in silence. All I can think about is James and Kate and that they will lose their father. Even though they are not close, it will still be a devastating loss.

***

The next few hours I attempt to work in my home office and return emails. I cannot concentrate. My thoughts keep returning to Vince and the fact that he is dying of cancer. I begin the process of keeping a journal, hoping it will help me manage my thoughts and emotions.

November 18, 2011

> *My heart aches for Kate and James. How will they handle this news? I am absolutely numb.*

I need a drink. A very strong vodka martini with blue cheese olives sounds really good right now. I wish I had someone who I could call, so I could escape for just a few hours. Someplace to run to and deny the suffocating knowledge that Vince is going to die. I just want to forget for a while.

Kate is out with friends, and I won't have to pick her up this evening. I can't find any vodka in the house, so I decide to open a bottle of cabernet. Two glasses in, my phone rings. It's James.

"Are you crazy?" he screams at me.

"What are you talking about?"

"I just overheard Dad telling someone that you and Kate are moving in?"

"Yes. We are. Your dad is very sick, and we think it is the best thing to do. This way you and your sister can spend time with him."

"You're divorced and you worked so hard to get divorced. Why would you want to live with Dad again? This is the stupidest idea! Does Kate know?"

"No. Not yet. We are having a family dinner on Sunday to discuss it."

"I won't be there. This is a really dumb idea. If you move in, I'm moving out. You and I can't live together. And where is everyone supposed to sleep?"

James and I have had a strained relationship through high school, so I am not surprised that he has no interest in living under the same roof again.

"James, you are just going to have to trust me. This is the best thing for everyone. Your father is going to need lots of help, and I don't want the burden to fall on you and Kate. "

My mind feels foggy. Too much wine and no food all day is not the best combination. I know James is worried that I will step in with a bunch of rules. I assure James that I am there to be Kate's parent, that he is a grown up and I no longer need to parent him.

After I hang up, I pour another glass of wine and sit on my bedroom floor. My primary concern is to make sure James and Kate have the opportunity to build a better relationship with Vince. They will have a chance to connect with him in a very different way than they have before. I will have to look past all the scars that were created when we were married. I will need to wear an invisible suit of armor against Vince's words.

A new fear begins to grip me. I am scared I may not be strong enough to stand up to Vince and his uncontrollable temper. Big heavy sobs come deep from within my heart. I again feel the pain of all the harsh words and broken promises of our marriage. I am buried under a blanket of painful emotions.

I come to the realization that I have only sadness to battle. My empathy for Vince begins to overshadow any anger or resentment I used to feel. No one deserves to die alone.

***

In the midst of packing my house, I also accompany Vince to all of his doctor appointments. Vince's local oncologist has a patient and calm demeanor and puts Vince at ease. We leave our first meeting with some hope that Vince will be able to buy some time.

I tell Vince that this would be a good time to sit down and discuss expectations and our financial arrangement before I move in. We are both hungry so we stop for some lunch at our local deli.

I am currently receiving child support for Kate and I am concerned with losing this financial support. I know that I will be spending quite a bit of time away from my work, helping Vince with doctor's appointments and taking care of him when he is sick. When I am not working I am not generating billable hours, so I am anxious about whether I will be able to continue to generate the revenue required to meet overhead expenses for the company.

Financial conflict has always been a theme in our marriage. I was privileged enough to be a stay-at-home mom; however, Vince always resented that I did not contribute financially to the household. I did my best to manage all aspects of family life and to support Vince and his career in anyway I could. I thought of us as a team. I took care of anything Vince needed so he could focus on his career. I often hosted last-minute dinner parties and manager meetings at our home. While we were married, I took great pride in caring for Vince and our family. These days, I joke that I would be so much more successful if I had a wife like myself.

"We should talk about our expectations of living together and what your expectations are financially," I say when we sit down to eat.

"You are doing me a favor, so I will pay for everything. I don't want you to worry about anything. I will take care of everything."

"Okay," I say, but deep down I am uneasy. Vince likes for people to know he has money and that his wealth was self-made. He is great at making grand gestures, but most of the time he rarely delivers on his promises, especially financial ones.

Early on in our marriage his gestures to pay for things generally never panned out. In the late '80s, I graduated from college, and began seeking interviews for jobs with advertising agencies. We were living in Baltimore, Maryland at the time, which did not have a large advertising market. I was extremely excited when I secured an interview with a top New York advertising agency with offices in Baltimore. I called Vince to share the news. I had just sent out my resumé earlier in the week. They called me on Thursday morning to schedule an interview for that afternoon. I was very young and had never been on a "real" interview. I asked Vince what I should wear.

"You need to go to the department store and buy a really nice grey or black suit. I'll pay for it as a graduation gift," he said. "Just open up a store credit card and charge it. I will pay the bill when it comes in. Good luck."

I appreciated his guidance. He had been working in a sales environment for six years and had far more experience than I did. I drove to the store, purchased a suit and made it to my interview in plenty of time. It was a beautiful grey suit that cost $325, a lot of money back then. I felt so professional and I am proud to say I was offered the job. Unfortunately, when the department store bill arrived, Vince had decided that since I was working, I should pay for my own suit. I was so hurt and too young and naïve to call him out on it.

These past experiences make me feel skeptical regarding Vince's new promise to take care of all of the expenses. For some reason, I feel the need to justify to him my need for continued financial help.

"I am concerned about losing your monthly support," I say in between bites of my sandwich. "I'm still paying off debt from James' boarding school tuition."

"Just tell me how much you need each month," he says.

I feel guilty asking for his financial assistance. If I were more successful, then I would not need to rely on his child support.

"Let me think about it," I say.

I wonder if Vince understands the sacrifice I am making for not only the children but also for him. I will be living in a 10-by-12-foot bedroom as a visitor in his house. The things that had made my own home feel like home will be packed away. I will not be able to date or have a social life while I live with him and the children. My life will be on hold.

CHAPTER TWO

DECEMBER — THE GIFT

December 18, 2011

> *Today is moving day. I haven't even had time to create closure with the home where I have raised my children for 16 years. With the help of many friends, we have packed a 5,000-square-foot home in 30 days. I sold every piece of furniture in our home within 24 hours. The only pieces we will take to Vince's are the children's beds and two special items.*
>
> *I am getting ready to turn my life upside down and I am sick with fear. I am trembling. I am so very scared that I will allow him to change me again. I am afraid I won't be able to handle the stress of watching someone who I was once close to die.*

The movers feverishly load the truck. Colored tags adorn the boxes, indicating whether they are for Vince's house, storage or donation. Some of my neighbors have stopped by to say goodbye. Everyone keeps talking about what a noble thing I am doing. Their acknowledgement and compliments make me uncomfortable. *Isn't this what anyone else would do?* Am I crazy for moving back in with someone that reduced me to a shell when we were married?

Our marriage wasn't always difficult. We had some very good years, especially the years while we were starting our family. Vince was attentive and really tried to be a good husband. But after a while, he began chipping away at my self-esteem little by little. As I think about this, I begin to have doubts about my decision to move in, but there is no time to stop.

"We are ready to go," a mover calls out. That's it. I switch off my feelings and operate on autopilot.

***

When we arrive at Vince's, he announces that he is leaving to run errands. It's just like Vince to disappear. My exhaustion is the only thing that tempers my anger. Even as I make this very grand gesture, he is incapable of supporting anyone but himself. I am incredulous that he can't even hang around to offer to pick up lunch for everyone. He could have ordered pizzas or picked up sandwiches. Instead, I am forced to pull Kate and her friends off their tasks of unpacking to get food.

I think Vince is feeling even more uncomfortable than I am. He doesn't deal with change very well. I'm moving in and changing his environment. That must put him on edge. Vince has never been one to consider other people's emotions or welfare. Today I am giving him a priceless gift. Certainly, he should be overcome with humility and want to be as helpful as possible, but his car vanishes down the street as the movers begin unloading our belongings.

Vince's departure has left me on the brink of tears. I have to hold it together for Kate, though. This is a good thing…moving in as a family while Vince dies. I tell myself that over and over again as I stand in the driveway directing boxes.

One of Vince's next door neighbors comes over to say, 'hello." She wraps her arms around me and gives me a big hug. My eyes once again swell with tears.

"You are an angel for moving in here. There are not many people who would do what you are doing."

20

I want to scream at the top of my lungs, "This is not my life. I'm living someone else's life. Doesn't anyone see that this isn't my life?"

I am really beginning to doubt how I will get through this. I feel so alone. I thank her for welcoming me. I inhale deeply and solemnly walk inside to begin this journey...our journey toward the light.

***

I spend the next two days unpacking. I am aware that clutter puts Vince on edge. I try to put everything away as quickly as possible. Every night I navigate through a forest of wardrobe boxes to get to my bed, which really isn't mine. My bed was sold with my home, so I sleep on the guest bed. The mattress is very old, and my room is an array of misfit leftover lamps and furniture. I feel so out of place.

***

Two days later, I return back to my old home to pick up some final items. Vince has insisted on coming with me so he can say goodbye to the house. *Didn't he say his goodbyes when he moved out seven years ago?* Why is he determined to encroach on my private moment? I am so angry. I go upstairs to begin checking for any items that have been left behind. I walk into Kate's bedroom and am overpowered with emotion. A flood of home videos begins streaming through my mind. I move from room to room, and the memories continue to overwhelm me. Sixteen years have gone by in the blink of an eye. I have that feeling I get when I've just finished reading a really good book. I wish I could go back and read it again for the first time.

***

In honor of Christmas, we have always decorated our house from top to bottom, giving each room a different theme: snowmen, Santa, holiday fruits and candies, and bears. I remember how much Vince loved having the house decorated for the holidays. Our 10-foot Christmas tree adorned with hand-blown glass ornaments was his favorite.

While Vince is away, I suggest to Kate that we decorate his house. Somehow I know that this will be his last Christmas with us. We dig through the storage garage and load all of the decorations, including the Christmas tree, into two SUVs for the ride to Vince's. I encourage Kate to take charge. I want this to be her very special gift to Vince.

Ever since the children were little, we'd made it a tradition to purchase a new hand-blown ornament for every member of the family at Christmas. I always choose something that represents a milestone from the past year. Each and every ornament on the tree has a special story behind it. The tree is adorned with glass soccer balls, horses, buildings from Italy and Chicago, all representing special moments for our family. This year I have decided to purchase an ornament for Vince...an angel. She is dressed in white and has blonde hair and an angelic smile. She represents faith and my desire that someone watch over him.

Decorating the tree takes several hours. I carefully unwrap each ornament and hand them one by one to Kate. She places them with care on the boughs. We add ribbons, silk flowers and a beautiful glass tree topper. The tree sparkles with hundreds of white twinkle lights and the hope of the holidays. Vince's house looks amazing. Every inch is wrapped in holiday cheer.

A parade of Santas marches up the stairway. Crystallized fruit garland swirls around the railings. Bright red holly berries adorn the doorways. Embroidered pillows with Christmas wishes hang from every knob in the house. Ornaments on ribbon dangle from tulle-covered chandeliers. And tulle and stockings line the mantel.

Kate waits in the living room for Vince to return. He walks in and is overcome with the glittering, sparkling lights of the season. He cries as he takes in the amazing gift his daughter has given him. This sets the stage for a Christmas focused on our reunited family.

***

We prepare to spend Christmas in Philadelphia with Vince's family. But before we leave, we plan to have Christmas at home, just the four of us.

This will be our first Christmas together in more than seven years. It is a simpler Christmas, unlike previous holidays, where we ate lavish meals and exchanged extravagant gifts. Vince's prognosis is not good, and we are aware that this may be his last Christmas with us. We want to spend it focusing on the important things rather than the material. I order a simple dinner from the local Italian restaurant. We eat and take turns watching each other unwrap small gifts.

Everyone appears a little uncomfortable, but we manage to have a few laughs. The kids eventually retreat to their bedrooms in the basement, and I am left alone with Vince. We are uncomfortable as we struggle to make small talk. I assure myself that the awkwardness will lessen as time goes on.

***

Vince comes from a large Italian family. During our marriage, I had always been the one to maintain our relationships with his family members. I was incredibly close to both his parents, especially his father. We spoke everyday by phone and we always ended the conversation with, "I love you." He passed away 13 years ago after a tragic complication from a knee replacement. After his death, I missed him terribly. I've often wondered if things would have ended differently for Vince and I if his father were still around. As I

23

write this now, I still feel a profound sense of loss, and I realize that Vince will soon see his father again.

Vince picks Kate and I up at the airport (James is scheduled to arrive later), and we go straight to his mother's house. The move has been grueling, and I am exhausted. I've thrown myself into participating in a family Christmas for James and Kate's benefit without even considering how I might feel. Now that we are at Vince's family home, I am having a tough time keeping my emotions in check, and I feel the old resentments and anger start to bubble up. I feel like I am having an out-of-body experience.

Everyone in Vince's family is welcoming, loving and gracious when I arrive. They include me in everything, and it is as if Vince and I never divorced. Unfortunately, this makes me even more uncomfortable. I try to make small talk. I busy myself with the tasks of cooking and then the cleaning up after meals, but my awkwardness persists. I am going through the motions, but no one even notices. This is going to be much harder than I imagined. I have not forgotten all the broken vows and promises of our marriage and I am drowning under the sad memories. I recognize that I will have to forgive and forget. Where do I even start?

CHAPTER THREE

JANUARY—THE CHEMO MONSTER

January 1, 2012

New Year's Day. I lie in bed breathing deeply, trying to slow my heartbeat. Traditionally, this is the day when people are all hung over after a long night of celebrating that the previous year has ended and a new year of promise stretches out before them.

This will not be a year of new beginnings for me. It will be one of the hardest years of my life. I am consumed with fear for all that will happen in 2012. I am scared of how I will handle continuing to live with Vince. I feel like a guest in his home and I can't seem to find a comfortable spot. My room is down the hall from his, and I am having trouble making it feel like a safe haven. My heart beats so very fast, and my chest feels so tight.

I drown in my emotions. I am sad for my children who will lose their father. He is much sicker than anyone knows. I am sad for Vince who will die far too young and will miss seeing his children become young adults and raise families of their own. I am terrified for myself. Will I handle all the pressure that Vince puts on me? Will I still be able to run a company, and most importantly, will I be able to take the best care of my children?

With our encouragement, James has decided to take a year off from school and live at home. At first, James did not agree with us; however, the timing could not have been better. Staying home this year will allow him to spend time with Vince. Even though they have been living together for several months, they have yet to learn to communicate with one another. Vince tries desperately to mold James into a version of himself. Most of their communications turn into lectures from Vince. These interactions leave James feeling like he doesn't measure up, and they widen the rift between them.

I think James believes that Vince does not deserve to have his family around him, because Vince made very little effort to keep his family together. James questions why everyone forgets—just because Vince is sick—all the things Vince has done to our family. James sees Vince's ego front and center. He knows that, even stricken with cancer, his father has not changed. James is a pragmatic young man, and he feels like Vince never gave him time or respect. Why should James now spend time with his father when the man never tried to be a dad?

James stays busy delivering sandwiches for a well-known sandwich shop. He works afternoon and early evening shifts five to six days a week, so he is able to avoid spending time with Vince. When he is home, he retreats to his own room in the basement and barely speaks to anyone. I am careful not to push James to engage with us too much. He and I have a very fragile relationship. I have been the disciplinarian in his life, and that has put me in a very unlikable role. I prefer to give James lots of space, now, and to let him make his own decisions.

Most afternoons, I find Kate lying on Vince's bed telling him about her day at school. When Vince was first diagnosed, I was very concerned about the pressure his illness would place on Kate. I did not want her to fall into a caretaker role. That would be far too much responsibility for a 16-year-old. I have assumed the role of caring for Vince, so that the children can enjoy as much quality time with him as possible. I think deep inside Kate knows her time with her father is limited, so she soaks up every minute with him. Each afternoon, I stop by his room on the way to my room to change. I sit in the large wingback chair next to his bed, and he, Kate and I gossip, laugh and often make plans for dinner. Kate drags her school books in and works on her homework while Vince reads or naps.

We have as many family meals together as we can, but James' work schedule often keeps him away at night. Kate has projects and school commitments that keep her occupied, as well. On these nights, Vince cooks occasionally, and he is always willing to pick up dinner when I am too tired to make it.

Vince relishes our family dinners. He has spent many years eating dinner alone, and having his family around the table now fills him with love. I dread the nights the kids are not able to join us. On these evenings, we almost feel like a couple, and I am incredibly uncomfortable. I never imagined I would be sharing nightly dinners with Vince after our divorce. As hard as I try, I cannot keep the memories of our marriage from sneaking into my thoughts.

I remember how I used to spend hours preparing delicious dinners from scratch. If we had salad, I would make my own croutons and salad dressing from recipes. However, the delicious home-cooked meals were never enough to entice Vince home. He preferred to have drinks after work with business associates. The memories of those rejections still hurt.

Kate and I research the type of foods cancer patients should eat. I try to cook meals that are healthy and rich in protein. Individuals with cancer need to consume lots of protein for strength. Esophageal cancer patients should avoid specific foods, especially those containing sugar, which feeds cancer cells. Unfortunately, Vince continues to attempt to eat things he shouldn't. He is angry when he can't complete his meal or has to vomit up food that has gotten stuck in his esophagus. Vince has always worked very hard to be in control of every aspect of his life. Eating what he wants, even though he shouldn't, is his way of not letting the cancer control him. The irony is that the cancer wins out every time. He just hasn't realized it yet.

***

Vince started chemotherapy in December and will continue to have chemo through the month of January. His hair began to fall out after just the first chemo treatment. He returned from the Christmas holidays almost bald. He looks pale and tired. The poisonous cocktail of drugs takes a toll on him.

Chemo days and the day immediately after are always the best days. The drugs take almost six hours to be pumped into his body. Part of his chemo cocktail includes steroids, which relieve the inflammation and make him feel almost normal. Another benefit of the steroids is that he is able to eat food without choking. On these days we gather as a family and chose a restaurant where Vince can enjoy a food he has been craving.

But then, after chemo, there are five days of excruciating pain that follow. He can barely walk, every muscle hurts, he feels pain deep inside his bones and he has the chills. He struggles to get food down. The kids and I try to pretend everything is normal, but normalcy is difficult.

On most nights Vince must lean forward in his chair, maximizing the small opening that is left in his esophagus. He must eat very slowly, take small bites and chew his food well. Lentil soup with risotto, an Italian rice, is one of Vince's favorite meals. I have read that soups are great for esophageal cancer patients, and I know lentils are packed with protein, so one night I make it, hoping it will provide him some energy. Unfortunately, as Vince begins to eat, the risotto lodges in his esophagus. He starts coughing and choking. He jumps up and barely makes it to the sink in time for the soup to explode out of his mouth. We all stop eating and clear the table in silence.

Everyone retreats to his or her own space not knowing what to say to Vince.

We are confronted everyday with Vince's cancer and the effects it has on his body. He sleeps until noon each day. He showers and then has a few hours of energy to spend time with the family before he is forced to nap until dinner.

We all try to do what we can to keep Vince comfortable. Kate and I watch TV with him most nights. Vince even watches some of the same television shows Kate likes. She has begun watching a teenage drama on ABC's family channel. It's about four high school girls who are trying to solve the murder of their best friend. I smile when I hear them talking about plot twists and what they think will happen next. Vince even knows the names of all the characters. James works most evenings, and if he is home, he chooses to watch TV in the basement alone.

***

I am surprised to see how Vince's cancer has made him a celebrity. It's created a "rock-star" effect. Friends, business associates and family members email and call daily. They share their shock and sympathy and they offer to help. Business associates laud his successful career and tell him that his sales leadership will be missed. Vince's cancer has allowed him to reconnect with people in his life that he has not spoken to in years. Sadly, his cancer has become his job. He is on everyone's radar, and his ego flourishes. I sit back and watch helplessly as he becomes his cancer.

One afternoon while Kate is busy with friends, I listen to several of these conversations. I watch as Vince lights up with each compliment. I am surprised when I begin to feel angry. I am mad that he is being applauded for a career that has always meant more to him than his family. I overhear him make plans to visit business friends, many of whom he has not kept in touch with or seen in quite some time. I moved in so he could finally put his children first while he still has time.

I am cognizant in this moment that nothing has changed. Faced with death, Vince will spend what time he has left talking and visiting with friends because this feeds his ego. I had hoped that he would want to spend as much time as he could with James and Kate, repairing their relationships. I wish he would focus on his family and soak up the love we provide. But love does not feed his ego.

The kids and I cannot give his ego daily praise, because the reality is that he was a terrible husband and an uninvolved father. He fails to realize that even though the children are distant, they have nothing but love for him in their hearts. Even though we are divorced, I have absolute empathy and compassion for him at this time. But his ego forces him to turn his back on us again as he makes plans to travel to see friends each weekend over the next several months. His focus is on his friends and acquaintances.

Old feelings of abandonment bubble to the surface, and my spirits sink. I am even more troubled to realize that I have not forgotten the past, which means I have yet to forgive. My heart begins to race, and I feel a sharp pain in my chest that takes my breath away. I rub my chest with my hand and attempt to massage the pain away. I try to breathe, but my chest feels tight and heavy. I can't listen to anymore of Vince's end of the phone calls, so I excuse myself. I head to my room to lie down and calm my racing heart.

***

The kids still have issues with their father, yet they seem to be adjusting to living under one roof. James and Kate enjoy having their bedrooms in the basement. It's almost like they have a little apartment. At one point, James even comments to Vince that "the house feels good, just like Mom." My heart swells when I hear this. I am encouraged by his response and know that I am doing the right thing for both he and Kate.

I make small changes each day to help make Vince's house feel more like a home for them. Vince does not like change, so I am met with resistance with even the most minor amendment. Vince had long ago turned the dining room table into an office with a printer, laptop and phone. Fortunately, the kitchen has a table for four, but it only has three chairs. I purchase four new kitchen chairs that coordinate well with the table. As I walk into the house carrying the first chair, Vince's annoyed expression says it all.

"Now we can all eat together," I say.

He does not say a word. I can tell he is miffed. I should have asked him if it was all right if I put new chairs in the kitchen, but deep down I knew he would say no. Having just three chairs does not make sense to me, since we are a family of four. This ends up being a much larger discussion than it needs to be.

Vince wants to eat at the dining room table, which would be fine except, as I pointed out, it doubles as his office.

"Just move everything when it's time to eat," he says.

"That seems like a waste of time and energy every night when we can just have four chairs in the kitchen."

"This is a waste of money." He turns and leaves the room.

When we moved, I brought a few things from our home for the kids' rooms, so they would feel comfortable. Even before I moved in, Vince had never spent any time making the kids' rooms in the basement feel homey, so I try now to add small touches here and there. Vince resists every addition. I am simply aiming to create a warm home environment, but he views any change as a loss of control.

My animosity begins to build. Vince's reactions remind me of when we were married. Whenever we needed a house repair, he would scream and yell at me about how much money it was going to cost.

***

I wake up every morning chanting, "I forgive," but it does not work. Forgiveness feels miles away.

I feel smothered by Vince's constant need to spend time with me. When we were married, if we spoke two sentences a week to each other that was a lot of communication. He hated coming home, and he reminded me of this fact every Friday. Now that we live under one roof again, he wants to talk to me all the time. After six years of living alone, he is so excited to have someone to talk to, even if it's me.

His constant conversation exhausts me. Why didn't he put this much effort into our marriage? Our conversations are one sided. I am incredibly guarded and have no intention of sharing what is going on in my life or career with Vince. He forfeited the ability to be a part of my life a long time ago. I am having a tough time letting him in, and I realize my forgiveness mantra each morning is not changing things.

***

I am so consumed with my own feelings that I don't realize James and Kate are struggling living with Vince, as well. On January 20th, 2012, it's clear I am not the only one having trouble adjusting.

It is a snowy day. I have spent the morning at my office, but I've rescheduled dinner plans with clients because of the sloppy road conditions. I work at my office until about 2 p.m. and then make my way home. It has been snowing all morning, and while there is little snow accumulation, the roads are a mess.

When I get home, Vince is napping in his room. He has had a rough day. Chemo side effects have begun, and he has the chills and excruciating bone pain. He has also developed a new condition. He is experiencing pain in his right leg from his sciatic nerve, and he can barely walk. Later, we will find out he has a tumor growing on his spine that presses on the nerve.

I arrive home to a quiet house. James and Kate are downstairs in their rooms, and Vince is upstairs sleeping. I open up the blinds in the living room and sit in the chair watching the snow gently fall. The view from the back of Vince's house is beautiful. Everything is blanketed in white.

Kate comes upstairs with her toiletries in hand to shower. She and I share the guest bathroom. Her brother has the bathroom in the basement. I decided early on that the two of them sharing a bathroom would be a disaster.

"Hey, what are you up to?" I call out.

"Just showering and then meeting my friends to hang out."

"It's snowing right now and it's suppose to snow through the night. You're not driving in these conditions," I say.

"What? You're kidding. What am I suppose to do then?"

"Stay in and have some family time."

"I don't want family time! I want to go out with my friends!"

"I'm sorry. I can't control the weather."

She storms off to her room in the basement without showering. Several minutes later I hear her brother speaking to her.

"Hey, what are you doing tonight?" he asks.

"Nothing. Mom said we can't go out because of the snow."

"She just means you can't go out because you are such a bad driver."

"No! That's not true, and she isn't going to let you go out, either."

"She can't tell me what to do. My car is my own. Besides, I hear Mom and Dad talk about what a bad driver you are all the time."

Kate is not a bad driver. James is just trying to aggravate her. It's working. She's fuming. I'm not sure who she is angrier with, me for not letting her go out or her brother for acting superior.

"Let's go ask her." Kate storms out of her room and runs up the stairs. James is close on her heels.

"Mom, James says he is going out tonight."

"James, you are not going out tonight. The roads are bad, and I don't want you driving your car."

"It's my car, and you can't tell me what to do."

The argument continues to escalate with James getting angrier by the minute.

Kate smiles. "See, I told you that you weren't going out."

James' face reddens until he explodes. He unleashes a torrent of hateful barbs at Kate that reduce her to tears. I jump to my feet and begin yelling at both of them to stop. I know that combatting yelling with more yelling is very ineffective, but we all make bad decisions occasionally. Kate storms off to the basement and slams her door. Moments later she bolts up the stairs with blood running down her arm.

"I slammed my fingers in the door," she says through sobs.

I grab her arm and move quickly to the kitchen sink so I can see what is happening. A large flap of skin hangs from her middle finger, and blood pours out. Her ring finger is already black and blue. I wrap the bloody finger in a clean towel and instruct Kate to hold it above her heart.

"You need stitches. We are going to the emergency room."

"What do you want me to do?" James asks, trying to be helpful.

"Nothing. Just take care of your dad while I am gone."

At this point James, Kate and I have calmed down. James and I focus on caring for Kate.

Just then, Vince comes to the railing outside his room. "What the hell is going on?"

I step under the rail where he can see me and tell him that Kate has hurt her finger and will need stitches.

"What? Oh my God!" Vince comes down as quickly as he can, dragging his leg.

"What the hell happened?"

"The kids were arguing. Kate slammed her fingers in the door. She needs stitches." I quickly pull on my snow boots and grab my purse.

Vince turns to James and begins raging. "This is all your fault."

My heart breaks for James as he faces yet another of Vince's tirades about being a bad brother, a bad son, a bad person.

I immediately come to James' aide, trying to protect him from Vince's hurtful words.

"Stop it right now!" I scream at Vince. "It was an accident."

James can no longer tolerate the barrage of horrible statements. He erupts.

Kate and I both scream at Vince and James to shut up and stop it.

"James, go downstairs!" I yell. "Vince, stop it. You aren't helping. Kate, get in the car."

"I'm driving you," Vince says, reaching for his car keys and hat.

"No. I'm driving her. I don't want you sitting in the ER with a compromised immune system. You're staying home. I will text you."

Kate and I make our way to the ER, which is usually a 20-minute drive. That afternoon it takes us almost 45 minutes. We arrive to a busy waiting area, but the hospital is able to triage Kate quickly and put her in a room. Unfortunately, it takes almost four hours for the staff to X-ray her, stitch her up and finally release her.

Kate and I spend our time together talking. She shares with me that she is feeling very stressed, sad and smothered. She and James are both having trouble living together. She knows moving in was the right thing to do, but she misses her old room and having her space. She confides how hard it is to come home every day and have someone in the house constantly.

"I thought you said I could keep my social life if we moved in together," she says. "I thought you wanted me to still do things with my friends."

I assure her that this is still the case. I realize that I need to step in and run interference with Vince for the kids, especially on the weekends. This was my idea to move in, and it is up to me to make sure the children are adjusting. I know it is incredibly important for both Kate and James to maintain their friendships and personal lives. I also know Vince will die eventually, and they will need their friends for support.

"I never have the house to myself," Kate continues. "Dad is always asking me what I'm doing on Friday and Saturday nights. He tries to convince me to stay in and spend time with him."

Kate shares with me that James feels the same way. Before Kate and I moved in, it was just he and Vince. James is used to answering to no one and having time alone, as well. Even though we are a family, we are not used to being a family. I have forced us to cohabitate like freshmen in a dorm. There is the messy roommate, who never cleans up and leaves his dishes everywhere. There is the neat roommate, who needs everything in its place. Another roommate creates drama and requires a lot of attention, and the last roommate is quiet and reserved and needs a lot of personal space.

I am aware that I have not done a good job of making sure the kids are feeling comfortable and adjusting to life together as a family. I need to put my own feelings aside and focus on James and Kate. I have the ability and responsibility to set the tone in the house. I need to spend more time with Vince on the weekends so the kids don't feel pressure to do so. It is important for them to maintain some sense of normalcy.

As Kate and I prepare to leave the ER, we stock up on dinner from the vending machines. It is 8:15 p.m., and we are both starving. We gather a dinner of pretzels, peanut butter crackers, peanut M&Ms and bottled waters. Kate's finger is bandaged, and for now she has no pain, thanks to all the Lidocaine shots to her finger.

I spend the long drive, assuring her that I will speak with her father. I promise her that she will have lots of personal time with her friends on the weekends. We slowly make our way through the snow-covered streets, neither of us eager to get home.

***

The next day, the snow has stopped. It's my birthday, and Vince has decided that we will have dinner together as a family. I am excited. It has been several years since both children were home at the same time for my birthday. I spend the afternoon in my room relishing some quiet time and reading. James comes to my room early in the afternoon to ask where I would like to eat dinner. I have been craving Chinese food, and there is a new Asian fusion restaurant in town. James heads off to let the rest of the family know where I have chosen to have my birthday dinner. He arrives back a few minutes later.

"Dad wants to eat at a different restaurant."

I can tell James feels bad that Vince has vetoed my request. I am disappointed that Vince is using James to manipulate me. Vince knows I will give in so that I don't create drama for James.

Not only does he try to assert control over the situation, but he also chooses a restaurant that will mean a long wait. Vince does not have patience for long waits, and he can barely eat. The thought of trying to eat at this particular restaurant on a Saturday night does not appeal to me. I am angry that on my birthday, Vince is still in control. I'm not sure why I am so surprised. This is typical Vince behavior. He puts his wants and desires ahead of anyone else's, especially mine. I just assumed this birthday would be different. After all, I have given him a priceless gift, quality time with his children. His behavior dredges up old feelings, and I try to push them down with my "I forgive" mantra. I defer to Vince's wishes because he is sick, and dinner is not worth the argument.

Kate spends the afternoon at a friend's house. James agrees to pick her up and meet us at the restaurant. Vince and I make the drive together in silence. The only thing that is special about the evening is that both of my children will be with me on my birthday. It's the best birthday gift. When

Vince and I arrive, the wait is more than an hour. We make our way to the bar and secure two stools. We each order a glass of wine and wait for our buzzer to vibrate. My phone rings. It's James.

"Hey, Kate and I are here but Kate won't come in. She has a migraine, and her finger really hurts."

"Where are you guys?"

"In the hallway right inside the mall."

I explain to Vince what is happening and tell him I will be right back. I find Kate sitting against the wall. She looks miserable and pale. After a very brief conversation, I send her home. Of course, that means James must leave, too, because someone must drive her. I walk back to the bar slowly, dreading spending my birthday evening with Vince alone.

"Now we can just eat here at the bar," he says.

I am beyond disappointed. The last person I want to celebrate my birthday with is my ex-husband. Not only are we eating at a restaurant that I did not choose, but now we are also eating at the bar. We order several appetizers. Vince laughs and chats away as if we are a couple on a date.

One of the results of moving in together is that everyone treats us like a couple, including Vince. I feel like I'm on a really bad first date where the guy talks about himself the entire time—one of those dates where you wish you had arranged for a friend to call midway through dinner with an escape excuse.

I am barely listening to the conversation when Vince suddenly turns serious.

"I still can't believe you agreed to move in," he says. "It's the most generous thing anyone has ever done for me. Just a couple months ago we could barely stand to speak to one another. I hope someday you will be able to forgive me for what a terrible husband I was."

I take a deep breath. "I forgave you the day I moved in, Vince. I had to. How else could we live together if I hadn't?" As the words leave my mouth, I am aware that they're a lie. My emotions are in conflict. I feel as if I must have forgiven him a little, otherwise I couldn't have moved in. But resentment shows up every time Vince's actions are insensitive.

I have always had the ability to take a really bad experience and "box it up" and "put it on the shelf." When I moved in with Vince, I thought I had packed all the emotions away. Instead, each day an old memory slips out and invades my thoughts. The more time Vince and I spend together, the more I am reminded that he has not changed. He's still taking his family for granted.

Vince orders several slices of cheesecake to take home. When we get back, we sit around the kitchen table with James and Kate and dive into our dessert.

That night as I climb into bed, my heart begins to race, my breath quickens and the tightness returns to my chest. Each time I take a deep breath, a pain grips my lungs. I'm worried.

CHAPTER FOUR

FEBRUARY — I WISH YOU WERE HERE

Vince has to head back down to MD Anderson in Houston, Texas, to meet with his doctor. When Vince was first diagnosed, one of his best friends and a fraternity brother put Vince in touch with a surgeon recognized for her research and treatment of patients with this type of cancer. She has had much success with re-sectioning the esophagus and stomach, giving patients the opportunity to prolong their lives by several years. The procedure is complicated, and the recovery period is intense and as long as 10 weeks. Patients who have the procedure must sleep sitting up so acid from the stomach does not rise and damage the new esophagus. If Vince has this surgery, he will also have to eliminate certain foods from his diet, like sugar and most fats. His stomach will be a small pouch, and he will have to eat little meals all day long to receive enough nutrition. The surgery will mean major life changes and a long recovery period in Houston. Vince is hopeful.

During Vince's initial visit to MD Anderson in December, two of his fraternity brothers joined him. Vince spent two days undergoing tests, and then on the last day, he met with his doctor. She gave him hope that if the tumors responded to the chemotherapy, he would be a candidate for surgery. Afterwards, he and his fraternity brothers discussed how Vince would live in Houston for his initial recovery. They made plans to attend future sporting events together and the first football game of the season for the University of South Carolina, Vince's alma mater. After that first visit, Vince returned energized and committed to buying some time. He then spent the month of January receiving chemotherapy every other week.

Vince, now back in Houston, has to have another PET scan to see if the cancerous tumors are receding.

Vince calls me late in the afternoon. I am at the eye doctor with Kate. My phone rings, and my stomach immediately knots up. Somehow I know the news will not be good. I step into the hall to take his call. I can barely hear him speak.

"Its bad." Vince starts to cry. "I really wish you were here."

We had originally planned to travel together to Houston. Up to this point, I had been attending all of his doctor's appointments with him. But when it came time to make the airline reservations, he decided that it was too expensive to purchase two tickets and pay for two hotel rooms. Vince has always been incredibly frugal. So he chose not to bring me with him.

"I was so stupid. I should have just bought you an airline ticket to come with me."

I don't think he ever even fathomed that there might be bad news. He fully expected to be scheduling a surgery date for March and making plans for where he would live during his recovery. I can only imagine how defeated and scared Vince is at this moment.

"You will be home tomorrow," I tell him.

"I don't think I can handle this, Karen. I really wish you were here to help me."

"You will be home tomorrow. We will get through this. Tell me what she said."

"I'm going to die. The cancer has spread. I have tumors on my spine, hip and liver. She can't do the surgery."

I can barely understand what Vince says through his sobs. *Why didn't he let me come with him?* No one should hear such devastating news alone. I offer to fly down that evening.

"No. I will be home tomorrow." And with that he hangs up. I walk back into the waiting room where Kate sits. I know she can read the emotions on my face, but I don't want to tell her what her father said.

"Was that Dad?"

"Yes." I say as cheerfully as possible.

"What did he say?"

"I told him we are heading into your eye doctor appointment and that I'll call him later."

On the way home, I share with Kate that Vince will be unable to have surgery.

For Kate, James and I, hearing that surgery is not an option is actually a relief. Vince had never even discussed with us his plan for his 10-week recuperation. I had periodically overheard him talking on the phone with friends. He'd say that his mother, the kids and I were going to take turns going to Houston to care for him while he convalesced. Vince is not a tolerant patient, and we knew this would be a strain on us all. I had no intention of sending the kids down alone to take care of him like he had planned.

At the time I overheard him talking about it, I was angry at his cavalier attitude. He believes that we should want to care for him, but he forgets that he has never cared for us in that way.

I've already started to feel like a cook and part-time nurse. Did he really expect us to take turns flying back and forth to Houston to take care of him? The answer was that, yes, in fact he did. He had been preparing to rent a one-bedroom apartment. Friends would listen to his plans and ask him where Kate, James or I would sleep.

"The sofa," he'd answer.

That evening as I try to fall asleep, my anguish for Vince overshadows my resentment. Suddenly, this is all very real. Vince is going to die. Even though we always knew this, it is still devastating to have an option eliminated.

***

I pick Vince up at the airport. He looks so pale. He can barely use his right leg. He is bent over and looks so broken. He appears much older than his 53 years. What do you say to someone who has just been given a death sentence?

"How are you doing?" I ask.

"Not so good."

"So tell me about your visit."

He tells me every detail, explaining the outcome of his PET Scan. He is confused by the fact that his chemotherapy is considered unsuccessful. The tumors in his esophagus and stomach have shrunk by almost 50%, but the cancer has started growing in other places. Just six weeks earlier those tumors had not even existed. It is common for the first round of chemotherapy to partially shrink the original tumors. He is on a special cocktail of chemotherapy using a drug that has shown great promise with esophageal tumors. Unfortunately, the growth of new tumors means that he is considered terminal. His cancer is aggressive and will ultimately consume his body. There will be no surgery.

The doctor explained that treatment at this point will continue to be palliative. She will work with his local oncologist and radiologist to keep him as comfortable and pain-free as possible. She recommended another round of chemotherapy to continue to shrink the larger original tumors and possibly the addition of a stint in his esophagus. Having a stint implanted would allow him to continue eating for as long as possible. She also recommended having a port installed to allow the doctor to administer chemotherapy that way, instead of through his veins. She expressed concern that his veins could deteriorate the sicker he becomes. A port would also allow his doctors to keep him hydrated should that become necessary.

Vince refuses to have the port installed. He wants to travel, and he worries that a port will be visible under his shirt and hinder any trips he has planned.

He goes on to share with me that his doctor had suggested that he radiate the tumors on his spine. They are beginning to cause chronic pain in his legs and lower back. Hopefully, the radiation will shrink these tumors and give him some relief from the unbearable pain. Early on we had decided that all chemotherapy and radiation treatments would be administered locally in Chicago where we live.

I am annoyed that he fights against many of the recommendations from the doctors. The majority of them would provide a better quality of care for him and make life easier for both of us.

"I really think you should consider having the port installed," I say. "I have talked to several friends who say it is great to have so when you really need hydration it is easier for them to administer."

"Look. It's my decision, and I don't want it," he says.

Once again, Vince is in absolute control and will not listen to anyone else. This behavior reminds me of our marriage, and some feelings of bitterness start to bubble up.

He takes out his phone and begins making calls to family and friends to deliver the news. He looks weary and very pale. My heart begins to beat rapidly, and I feel the same sharpness in my chest.

***

That night after dinner, I gently broach the subject with Vince of Kate's college visits. He has decided that he will accompany her to the University of South Carolina, his alma mater. While they are in the south, she will also visit the University of North Carolina and Wake Forest. I am very concerned about Vince making this trip alone with Kate. He looks so pale and tired. The chemotherapy is really taking a toll. He is sleeping more than usual. I wonder if depression is settling in or if the cancer steals his energy. I know this trip is very important to Vince, but I am afraid the travel may be too exhausting for him. The hard truth is that he will not be around to see Kate go off to college or even graduate from high school. He is determined to make this trip happen for that very reason.

"Hey, I was thinking, if you want, I can fly down with you and Kate this weekend for her college visits." I say.

Vince's first reaction to anything I say is always, "No!"

He looks worn out. I wonder how he will manage all the walking with his right leg in chronic pain.

"I can tag along just in case you get tired. I'll let you and Kate attend all the visits on your own. I can do all the driving and just be there for back up. You know, make things easier for you." I don't want to take away from his time with Kate, but I am really worried about how he will manage getting up early and all the walking that is involved with a campus tour.

"I'll be fine. Please just let me do this with Kate."

Several nights later Kate expresses her apprehension about traveling alone with her father. She is afraid that he is too sick and she won't know how to take care of him. He is having chemotherapy tomorrow, and the side effects generally settle in 48 hours later, just in time for their trip. She is worried that he will not have enough energy to get through the entire weekend, and she begs me to come along. I approach Vince again and ask him to reconsider, but he is adamant that he and Kate do this alone.

***

They depart on a Thursday afternoon for South Carolina. Kate has a tour scheduled for Friday morning. Fortunately, the flight is easy and uneventful, and they pick up their rental car at the airport. It is very late as they make the drive to Vince's best friends' home. That evening Kate texts me. She has arrived safely, and things are going well. I breathe a deep sigh of relief. Just maybe things will go smoothly.

Unfortunately, Friday morning is a completely different story. The texts begin to roll in early, and Kate gives me all of the details.

It is raining, and Vince is freaking out. He completely melts down when things do not go as expected. He is overwrought and worried he will get sick if he gets wet. He refused to bring an umbrella, so he and Kate are now standing in a parking garage while rain pours down. I am angry that his poor planning is impacting their visit.

"Kate. I don't know where to go. I can't get wet. Oh God, what am I going to do?" he says in between sobs.

The irony of this situation is that Vince is hysterical worrying he will get sick from getting wet; however, at home he refuses to use just basic hand-washing precautionary measures to ward off germs. Each time James, Kate or myself enter the house we immediately wash our hands with antibacterial soap so we do not spread any germs we have picked up. Vince refuses to follow the same procedures.

Kate is forced to assume the parental role in the situation. She is a problem solver by nature and immediately takes out her iPhone and pulls up the name of the building where the tour starts. She copies the address into her map function and asks for walking directions. Just then, a young woman walks by. Kate asks her for directions.

"Dad, come on. I know where to go," Kate announces and sets off. It is still pouring rain, and they both get soaked. They need to reach the administration building where the tour starts. Vince rails at God the entire way.

"Why are you doing this to me, God? Why? Why? What have I done to you?" he cries.

Once they arrive at the administration building, Vince tells Kate he won't be able to stay for the tour. He is wet and needs to change his clothes so he doesn't get sick. Kate is heartbroken. My next text from Kate is terse. She wants to know why I didn't come.

"Dad just left me alone at my tour. He is crying because it's raining and he got wet. He told me to call him when I'm done and he will pick me up."

She is disappointed and angry. My heart breaks for Kate. College tours are supposed to be fun, not filled with drama. I remind her that this is *her* college visit. Choosing a school is ultimately her decision, and maybe she will have an unbiased view of the school if her dad is not with her. I encourage her to enjoy herself, but I can't help but feel guilty she is alone.

Within the hour, the rain stops and the tour begins after a brief introduction. Kate texts me throughout the tour, telling me how beautiful the campus is and how nice the facilities are. She is excited and can picture herself as a student there.

Vince has really been pushing her to attend the University of South Carolina, so I am relieved she is having a positive experience. I think it was always his dream to have one of his children attend his alma mater.

He really had hopes that James would attend, but he has chosen the University of Cincinnati. He has deferred his acceptance until the fall. He is trying very hard to be his own man and make his own decisions. I think James wants to have an experience that will not be colored by Vince's constant negative commentary and judgments. I can't blame James, and I completely support his decision to choose a different college.

In South Carolina, the rest of the weekend is filled with more rain, and Vince begins experiencing the side effects of his chemotherapy. Kate tries to make the best of their weekend together. They travel to Wake Forest on Sunday and drive through the campus. It is raining, and Vince is so tired; they do not get out of the car.

I regret that I did not insist that I go along with them. I could have made the trip much easier on Vince. I understand his ego's need to be independent and to control the weekend, but this weekend is about Kate and her experience. Vince once again misses the opportunity to show the kids that they are more important.

On Monday, Kate has a tour scheduled at the University of North Carolina. They awake in the morning to more rain. Vince again takes it personally and asks God why he is punishing him.

Punishment is a constant theme in Vince's life. He has never accepted the fact that he cannot control anything except his own actions. Anytime something difficult happens, he takes it as a personal attack. I find it draining trying to reason with someone who believes God is out to hurt him. I have always assumed that God is busy with larger problems. Vince is not feeling well, and he is very concerned that they will have to fly home in wet clothes. So they leave the tour early.

***

On February 20th, 2012 Vince begins three weeks of radiation. His treatments are five days a week for 20 minutes each. The treatments themselves are easy and painless. Vince is actually able to drive himself to all of his appointments. His continued ability to drive will become a critical marker of his independence.

The radiologist is focused on shrinking the tumors around the top of his spine, which are causing weakness in his arm. Unfortunately, to effectively radiate these tumors, the technician needs to radiate from the front and the back of the neck. They try to minimize the impact to his esophagus, but the radiation must pass directly through his esophagus.

***

That same week I continue to suffer from a racing heart and sharpness in my chest. I am at the office, and each time I take a breath I am met with a sharp pain. I can no longer ignore my symptoms. I call my primary care physician and schedule an appointment right away. They check my vitals. My blood pressure is unusually high. I have suffered from low blood pressure my entire life. So low that I often get dizzy or feel faint if I move too quickly.

They hook me up to a heart monitor and draw blood. The good news is I have not suffered a heart attack. They call the hospital and schedule an EKG and stress test for that afternoon. I am also required to wear a Holter heart monitor to record my arrhythmia. I am to return to my primary physician for the results the next day.

February 27, 2012

> *I tried to sleep last night, but my heart continued beating so quickly. The heart monitor is so uncomfortable. I am so worried that something is wrong with me. I try to push the thought out of my head. I am too young and too healthy to have heart issues. I keep telling myself that I will be fine but I can't help but worry. I must keep myself healthy, so James and Kate will have at least one parent. The more I think about how they will only have me eventually, my heart races even quicker. I breathe deeply. Please stop.*

I am anxious when I arrive to see my doctor. I am so busy working and caring for Vince and the children, I hope the doctor realizes that I don't have time to be sick. My doctor is familiar with my living situation because Vince is his patient, as well. He begins by asking me about my schedule and stress level. My test results demonstrate that I have a very healthy heart. He informs me that I am suffering from Supraventricular tachycardia (SVTs). I am experiencing rapid heartbeats that can sometimes feel uncomfortable with tightness or sharpness in the chest. He believes stress is causing anxiety, and my body is reacting. I am so relieved that nothing serious is wrong, but how am I going to change my stress level? He prescribes anti-anxiety medication and sleeping pills.

The next day I attempt to take one of the anti-anxiety pills, but it makes me feel like I am in a fog. I can barely get any work done. Clearly, medication is not the answer. My health is at stake, so I know I need to find an alternative solution. My emotions about my current situation and the feelings that still haunt me from the marriage are impacting my health.

For my own well-being, I must forgive Vince for the past. How am I going to do that?

CHAPTER FIVE

MARCH — SUNBURNED

Vince's ego soaks up all the attention surrounding his cancer. He and I spend a lot of time talking about all the various people who reach out to him on a daily basis, either through email or with phone calls. He beams when he tells me about business colleagues who have praised him for influencing their lives. Vince feeds off the stream of attention, but he also feeds it. Every time he receives bad news from the doctor or experiences a setback, Vince immediately gets on the phone to share the information with everyone. He realizes that if he tells people he is feeling good, the attention disappears. So, instead, he focuses on the pain and suffering.

I know we, his family, don't feed his ego, so spending time with us does not fulfill him. The kids and I discuss his illness openly with him, but we choose not focus on it. We do not gush compliments about what a great father or husband Vince has been. We simply don't have those experiences to draw from.

***

Vince plans his yearly trip to the Big East Tournament in New York. He usually meets his uncle, two cousins and a close friend for a long weekend. He is determined to go this year, even though he is feeling run down.

"I want to make it to one last Big East tournament," he says.

He is excited to leave and is happy he is not feeling any side effects from the radiation yet. He makes the flight to New York but arrives very tired and begins experiencing a minor burning sensation in his esophagus. He rests quite a bit in his hotel room that first day, and we talk often on the phone.

He fills me in on all the family gossip and tells me about all the wonderful emails he continues to receive from business colleagues. His phone calls are emotionally exhausting for me. I am so tired of hearing what a wonderful colleague he was. I just want to scream, "Great, good for you. You were such a great co-worker that you neglected your family." Today forgiveness is far away.

Vince is excited to be at the tournament, so I try to focus on being happy for him. I can't help but feel discouraged that he continues to choose time away from the children. This weekend would have been a great opportunity for him to bring James along. Instead, Vince chooses to spend the time with friends and extended family.

He is able to attend all the games he wants to see. The kids and I even catch a glimpse of him on TV. It's a great weekend for Vince, except that the burning in his esophagus progressively worsens.

Vince and his group go to an Italian restaurant. Unfortunately, Vince cannot eat. The burning in his esophagus is more than he can endure. It feels as if he has a sunburn inside his throat. He drinks liquid Lidocaine in these situations to minimize the pain, but it provides little relief.

He calls me the next day. He is whispering and I can hardly hear him.

"I'm not feeling too good, Karen," he says. "My throat is so sore. I can barely swallow. It feels like I'm swallowing razor blades. I don't think I can handle this. Last night we went to dinner and I couldn't swallow my *cavatelli* (a type of pasta). I had to excuse myself and go to the bathroom to cough it up. I'm not sure how much more of this I can take. I'm in so much pain."

"Are you drinking the Lidocaine and taking your pain medication?" I ask, but I know the answer already.

"Yes. It's not helping. I finished what I brought with me. I had the doctor call in another prescription. I'm never having radiation again. Even if they tell me I could survive 10 more years if I had it, I would say no. This is the most miserable experience. The pain is excruciating."

Vince and I had read an article in December about a famous writer for *Vanity Fair* who had the same type of cancer as Vince. He described in graphic detail his journey through radiation and chemotherapy. It sounded horrific. As Vince shares how he is feeling, I think about passages from the article. Dread washes over me as I remember how the author suffered through treatment only to ultimately die.

From the beginning, Vince and I have discussed his wishes for treatment. He chooses to have a good quality of life versus quantity of life. He would prefer to live comfortably and pain free for as long as he can. He does not want to spend weeks and months in bed sick from chemotherapy and radiation. It is more important for him to spend time with his family and friends.

"I can't do anymore radiation, Karen," he says.

"I know. Can I do anything to help you?"

"No."

"You will be at your mother's house later today, and you can rest and maybe have some chicken soup?" I say, trying to comfort him. "Maybe that will be easier to get down?"

This weekend has not turned out as he had planned. His hopes are shattered, and I am frustrated that he has once again had unrealistic expectations. He is running himself into the ground with this weekend away. I am concerned he will pick up an infection with the airplane travel, germs and his compromised immune system. But, I hear the disappointment and sadness in his voice and I can't help but have empathy.

Later that evening I check on Vince. I want to make sure he is at his mother's and most importantly that he has consumed some calories, especially protein.

"How are you feeling? Did you drink an Ensure this afternoon?"

"I feel like shit. I haven't had anything to drink."

"Please, try to drink an Ensure. The protein will give you some energy, which will make you feel better."

"I have to go buy some," he says.

I am so confused. I had spoken with Vince's mom last week to explain to her what type of foods Vince should be eating. I also asked her to purchase Dark Chocolate Ensure Protein Plus drinks for him. I explained that bread and pasta stick in his esophagus, so he should eat eggs, soups and cooked vegetables. These foods are the easiest for him to swallow right now. I don't understand what happened and why there are no protein drinks for him. I am furious. I feel like I am the only person working to keep him healthy during his treatments. I am angry that I wasted my time calling ahead. The responsibility of caring for him from Chicago is taxing.

"This trip has been a total waste," he says. "All I wanted to do was come back east and eat all my favorite foods. And now I can't eat at all. Why does God punish me like this?"

I am dealing with a child, and his petulance is exhausting. I have not experienced what Vince is going through. I don't know what it is like to lose control of your life and not be able to eat your favorite meals. But the more he resists eating the right foods, the weaker he becomes and the harder the cancer attacks his body. I'm so tired of the same conversation. This is not the first time we have discussed the importance of eating the right foods to keep his energy high. I am so worried about him, but his resistance has pushed me to the edge. I decide that I will no longer nag Vince about his meal choices. Unfortunately, this does not relieve my frustration. He continues to complain about how horrible he feels. And I know that he would feel better if he could increase his energy level with healthy eating.

***

When he returns from the trip, he is angry and frustrated, and he begins taking it out on all of us. Everything upsets him. The smallest challenge causes an eruption of emotion. He is abrupt and short all the time and never misses an opportunity to lash out at James. Both children start spending more and more time away from home. I even begin spending more time in my room. He is driving us all away with his anger. It's beginning to feel like old times. Constant anger and raging. I know he is scared. His fear feeds his anger, but the three of us are giving up our lives to take care of him.

One Saturday morning while I'm at my office meeting with my business partner, I receive a text from Kate. It reads, "Dad threw up all over himself and he is freaking out. He is screaming at me to help him, and I don't know what to do." I text back that I will be home immediately. When I arrive home, I find Vince sleeping in his room. I check in with Kate, and she relays the events of the morning.

"Dad went to get coffee and a muffin and he was eating it in the car on the way home. The muffin got stuck in his throat, and he started coughing and threw up all over himself in the car. He came into the house screaming at me to help him. Mom, I didn't know what to do. There was vomit on him and all over the floor. I asked him what he wanted me to do and he screamed at me, 'Use your head Kate. Help me.' I didn't know what he wanted me to do. Why is he eating muffins? He knows those get stuck, and why would he eat in the car?"

I hug her. "I am so sorry you had to deal with that."

"I have to get out of here. I'm going to my friend's. I'll check in, but I'm not coming home for dinner."

Even Kate is choosing to have less interaction with Vince. He is driving us all away. I had forgotten just how much energy is required to live with Vince's ego. He has let down our children again. I am so tired of Vince choosing behaviors that create drama. Doesn't he realize that his outbursts are not normal, and none of us want to deal with him when he is raging. I am angry with myself for thinking his illness would change him.

The next week brings more emotional outbursts. One night at midnight, I hear a large bang. Vince starts screaming.

"Why? Why? Why? Why me, God? Why do you do this to me?"

My heart races, but I don't dare leave the security of my room. His emotions are out of control. I wish he would take his anti-anxiety medication, but he refuses because it makes him sleepy.

***

Kate and I prepare for our annual spring break trip to Marco Island, Florida. We have spent the last few spring breaks there with many of our friends. Vince, however, has other plans in mind. When we were married, the kids and I were never allowed to take spring break because it was always the same week as the close of Vince's business quarter. When the kids were younger, Vince would allow me to take them to visit his family or spend a night or two in downtown Chicago or Wisconsin. The year I filed for divorce, I planned our very first spring break to Florida. Every year since, we have either taken a cruise to the Caribbean, gone to Barbados or spent a week at the beach. I made sure the kids always had the opportunity to have spring break just like their friends.

Ironically, this year Vince decides he wants to go on spring break with us. I am shocked. I am not happy that he will be with us. Kate spends the majority of her time with her friends, so this means that Vince and I will be spending time together. Ultimately, by the time spring break arrives, he is too weak to travel. I am able to convince him that it does not make sense to travel if he will spend most of the day sleeping in his hotel room. James is busy working, so he will stay at home with Vince. Even though Vince's energy is low, he is still very independent. He is able to drive, get his own meals, shower and take care of himself.

Kate and I fly to Florida and embrace our break from Vince. She enjoys her days on the beach and evenings hanging out with her friends. I soak up the sun and relish the quiet solitude of being on my own. I work and manage to read a couple of books.

March 28, 2012

> *I am sleeping better than I have in a long while. I am so relaxed. Spring break with Kate is exactly what I need. The break from Vince has allowed me to recharge my batteries. I am enjoying running on the beach and having a lot of alone time. Kate is having such a great time hanging out with her friends. I am feeling energized and very happy.*

***

The last day of our trip we have a full day by the pool. Our flight isn't until later in the evening, so we spend the morning together relaxing. As we float around in the water, Kate sheepishly brings up the subject of home.

"I'm not looking forward to going back tonight," she says. "Dad is always so angry. The littlest thing sets him off. When we first moved in, he seemed happy to have us there. He always wanted to watch TV with me and now he doesn't. When he asks me to get something, if I don't move quickly enough, he yells at me. If I ask him a question, he yells at me. When you're not home, he expects me to take care of everything and help him. I don't like living with him anymore."

I am dismayed. I had no idea things had deteriorated so badly. I can only imagine how James must be feeling. He bears the brunt of most of Vince's tirades.

I thought living together would be a good thing for the kids, a chance for them to spend quality time with their father. We have all sacrificed our lives to move in. I have put my entire life on hold. I no longer date and rarely spend time with my friends. Vince is taking it all for granted again and taking out his anger on the wrong people.

I assure Kate that I will speak with Vince. She asks if I would be willing to move out. I assure her that, if that is the best solution, I will make it happen. I moved in with Vince for the children, and now that they don't want to live with him, I have no choice but to move out.

The kids love Vince because he is their father, but they do not have a deep bond with him. They are not willing to be his emotional punching bag. We have lived six years without yelling, screaming and raging. Kate and I have lived alone the last three years while James was away at boarding school. The drama is too much for Kate. Frankly, it is too much for me.

I empathize with Vince. I have no idea what it is like to wake up every morning knowing that you are dying. I know his anger is his way of asserting his life against the cancer. It must be dispiriting to live in a constant state of limbo, not knowing when the end will come. He is bitter that he has worked hard his entire life to make money, just to have his existence cut short. He is angry that he won't see his kids get married and have kids of their own. I truly feel sorry for him.

However, Vince made choices long ago that put his family at the end of his list of priorities. He has done very little over the years to build a healthy relationship with James and Kate. He cannot expect them to suddenly put their lives on hold to spend time with him. His cancer does not erase the past and is not an excuse to treat his family poorly.

Kate has had enough. She wants a game plan. We float around in the pool for several hours talking about getting an apartment that is large enough for the three of us: James, Kate and me. She wants to know how soon we can move out. I assure her that I will work as quickly as possible, but it could take up to a month. I promise her that if things continue to deteriorate, that we will move to a hotel. My primary responsibility and concern is for James and Kate. If this living arrangement is creating too much stress for them, then we need to make a change.

"Dad is going to be really mad," Kate says.

"Yes, he will be, but he really should be angry with himself for wasting this opportunity he has been given. I don't really care whether he is angry or not. My concern is that you and James are happy and healthy." I float towards her and give her a hug. She smiles at me. She knows I have her back. She recognizes that she and her brother are my priority. She is confident I will protect them.

Any empathy I have for Vince begins to turn to anger. He is taking us all for granted. Very few people have the opportunity to plan for their deaths. Even fewer people have the opportunity to reunite with their families and mend broken relationships. I have given Vince a priceless gift, and I am furious that he is wasting it and taking his children for granted yet again.

I feel defeated. I feel guilty for making a bad choice for our children and am overwhelmed at the thought of packing and moving again.

CHAPTER SIX

APRIL — PROMISES

Kate and I return from our vacation. This was the first spring break that Kate had wanted to leave the day her break began and not come home until the very last day. She wanted some distance from Vince and the cancer. I was happy to stay away as long as possible. When we return, we jump right back into our routines.

She heads back to school, and I head back to the office. Our first day back, I receive a text from Kate late in the afternoon asking if she can hang out at her friend's house. She promises to be home in time for dinner. James is at work. Perfect timing. I pack up my laptop and head home to speak with Vince. I dread the difficult conversation that I must have with him. I do not like confrontation, especially with Vince. But I know I must stand up for James and Kate.

When I arrive home, he is sitting in the living room watching a cooking show and reading the newspaper. He loves to read the paper, but his eyesight is beginning to fail. He is experiencing double vision, so reading an entire article is time consuming. I sit in the chair directly across from him.

"How was your day?" I ask.

"Not great. I'm not feeling too good. Where is Kate? Shouldn't she be home from school by now?"

"She went to hang out with friends. She will be home for dinner."

"She just got back from 10 days of hanging out with friends in Florida. Shouldn't she come home and spend time with me?"

"We need to talk," I say.

I take a very deep breath and remind myself to be strong and confident and to not let him bully me. He goes for the emotional jugular every time, and I am left with a gaping wound, flesh flapping and blood pouring out. I decide to try a new tactic. Instead of coming at him right away, I sympathize with him. Hopefully, I can diffuse the ticking time bomb that is inside him.

"I'm really sorry you weren't able to come on spring break, but it really worked out for the best. I hardly saw Kate and I worked most of the time. You would have been miserable just hanging out in your hotel room all day," I assure him. "She will be home for dinner."

"Do you want to order food?" he asks.

"That would be great. So your week seemed to go smoothly, and you're feeling pretty good?"

"Yes. I did have to go to the store twice, though, because James keeps drinking all of the Gatorade."

The drink issue has been brewing for months. Vince drinks Gatorade to replenish lost electrolytes and stay hydrated. James likes to drink sports drinks, as well. Kate and I drink water, so we manage to remain out of the conspiracy. I am so tired of hearing Vince yell and scream when he opens the refrigerator. We are living as a family, and we are responsible for buying the groceries for our teenage children. It is disheartening that Vince chooses to spend his last days with James arguing with him about Gatorade. We are not on a fixed budget, and providing hydration for our teenagers will not create a hardship.

I have a much more important conversation to have, so I decide to table the drink conversation.

"Having us all living together under one roof must be really hard for you?" I say.

"No. I really enjoy having you all here. You have really warmed up the house. It feels like a home now. I love spending time with Kate every afternoon."

"Really?" I ask. "I'm surprised to hear you say that."

Vince looks at me quizzically. "It's been really great having everyone under one roof."

"I'm really confused, then, because none of us feels like you appreciate us being here."

He looks at me with shock. "What do you mean?"

"The whole purpose of us moving in here was so the kids could spend quality time with you and hopefully repair or rebuild their relationships with you. But your constant meltdowns are creating an incredible amount of stress for us all. You have to remember that Kate and I have lived alone for the last few years. Our home was very peaceful. The last month has been unbearable. Every interaction is filled with anger, and you are raging again."

"I am not," he bellows.

Here we go again, I think, just like when we were married. Only this time it is different. I am stronger and know that I must stand up for James and Kate and what is right. I am no longer the broken woman afraid to use her voice. I take a deep breath. The truth is, he doesn't even realize how over the top and outrageous his behavior is.

"Have you noticed the kids are never around anymore?" I continue. "Have you noticed that I spend longer days at the office and have stopped watching TV with you at night? Did you notice that I go to bed earlier? Have you noticed that Kate spends all her time in her room? Have you noticed that James does not come home after work?"

I take another deep breath. He is seething with anger, and I can tell he is ready to unleash a torrent of rage. I have to strike quickly before he blows.

"Kate spoke to me on spring break and she has asked about the possibility of us moving back out."

Vince is stunned. All the angry red color drains from his face. He sits in silence.

"I moved in here so you could show James and Kate how much you love them," I continue. "I know you do, but your actions are creating a different reality. Have you noticed that no one talks to you anymore?"

He continues to look shocked. I am not surprised that he is completely unaware of how he is impacting all of us.

"That's too bad," I say. "I can't imagine what it is like for you to wake up everyday knowing you have cancer and are dying. But you have to stop being so wrapped up in yourself. You don't even see how you are affecting people around you. Anytime someone tries to speak with you, you shut them down and become short and hostile."

I take another deep breath. I must keep going. I owe this to James and Kate. This is the last chance Vince will have to choose his family. I have made it so easy for him to have his family back, and he is taking it for granted all over again.

"You've been given a gift, Vince. You have been given a second chance with your children. Something I thought you would never get. It's too late for you and I, but it's never too late to build new relationships with your children. You do not have the right to emotionally abuse any of us anymore. I'm sorry that you have to deal with this cancer. It's got to be incredibly hard, but you cannot take out your anger on your family. It is probably time for you to see a psychologist or join a support group to help you manage your emotions."

"I do not need to see anyone," he says, "and I don't need to join a support group. I'm fine."

Even now, faced with eminent death, his ego is still running his life. I feel defeated. I am so disappointed that I am unable to show him how to love from his heart. His ego wins. I can do nothing more.

"Very well," I say. "Have it your way. You know, Vince, life is about choices. We cannot control what life hands us; we can only control how we choose to react."

I look in his eyes for the first time in a very long time. I want him to understand how serious I am.

He sits back in his chair and smirks at me. Vince has the look of victory plastered across his face. He is remembering the old Karen who let him walk all over her. He has no idea how much I have grown and changed since our divorce. I am much stronger.

I remember the day I told him we needed to attend marriage counseling to save our marriage. I told him, that if he didn't show up, I would divorce him. He never showed for the appointments and just assumed that I had dropped the subject. Eventually, I told him I had been going to marriage counseling without him and that I'd filed for divorce. He was shocked. He never really believed I would gather the strength and courage to divorce him.

"So," I continue, "you will understand if the kids and I move out. I will not subject our children to your temper tantrums and raging behavior any longer. I gave you an opportunity to show James and Kate how much you love them, and you are wasting it. I am so disappointed. I hate that you are dying, but we are fortunate that we know you are ill. Imagine if you'd died suddenly of a heart attack.

"I will call my real estate broker, and we will be out by the end of the month. I will be asking James to come with us. I'm sorry this didn't work out. I guess I overestimated your desire to have your family around you."

The color drains from his face, but he still wears his smirk. I stand up and stare him right in the eye so he knows I mean business.

"I should make some phone calls," I say and head upstairs.

I really don't need to make calls, but I know if I stay, he will think there is room for discussion. I am done talking.

Thirty minutes later, I put on my running gear and headphones and go out for a long run. Tears mingle with sweat. I am so angry with myself for believing that Vince would change when faced with his mortality. I'm such a fool, and now I am worried I have done even more damage to the kids and their relationship with Vince. This will feel like a divorce all over again for everyone. How harebrained I was to think this would work.

***

"Did you have a good run?" Vince asks when I return.

"Yes," I say. I always feel guilty working out because I know Vince no longer has the strength.

"We are ordering dinner from the Italian place. James is home, so he will pick it up. Just let me know what you want."

I give Vince my order and head upstairs to shower. I am avoiding him. I am emotionally worn out. I have nothing left to give at this point.

At dinner, Vince is upbeat and tries very hard to make conversation with everyone. He acts as if nothing has happened. He chats all the way through the meal. I refuse to engage in conversation or even look his way. He tries to pretend that everything is fine, but there is tension in the air. After dinner as I clear the table, Vince asks if he can speak with me.

We sit across the room from each other in matching brown suede chairs. My body language is clear. I sit with my knees pulled up, not wanting to communicate.

"I don't want you and the kids to move out," he says. "Living together has been the happiest time of my life. You have given me the greatest gift, and I am sorry that I have taken it for granted. Please don't move out. You have been with me since the beginning, and I need your help. I can't imagine getting through this without you. I love seeing the kids everyday. I never knew how much I was missing until you moved in. I promise to treat you and the kids better."

"I appreciate your apology, but you're just spouting words," I say. "Stop telling me you are going to change. Just do it. The kids deserve better than what you are giving them, and if you can't give them better, then you will have to face this on your own."

"I understand."

***

Over the next few weeks, Vince attempts to control his temper, and when something upsets him, he tries to take it all in stride. I know he will be unable to sustain this long term, but I trick myself into believing that this time will be different. Upon reflection, it is easy to pretend I have forgiven him when his emotions are in check. I focus on his efforts and bury the past.

I realize that everyone feeds off my energy and that I can set the tone just with my disposition. Each day when I pull into the driveway, I take a very deep breath and put on a smile before I enter the house. I remind myself that I have a very important role to play.

Vince sleeps more these days. Most afternoons he remains in bed resting or reading the paper. I go upstairs to change my clothes and stop in Vince's room to talk with him for a little bit. This seems to put him in a better mood. I also spend more time with the children one on one and check in with them frequently. James continues to be distant, but I try to connect with him as often as he will let me.

***

Spring is in the air, but deep inside I am becoming resentful that I am working so hard. Vince is so consumed with his own needs. He does not behave as the other adult parent in the house. I wish he would put the children first and work alongside me to create a happy, stress-free, loving environment.

One night after dinner, Vince and I sit in the living room. He watches TV, while I stretch out on the floor with my laptop and pay my personal bills.

"Do you have work tonight?"

"No. Just paying bills," I say. "I was thinking we should get your bills set up online so when it gets hard to write checks, I can sit next to you and help you pay them. It's so much easier to pay online, and you don't have to deal with the envelopes."

Paying bills has always been a dramatic affair for Vince. He never seems to get the bill in the envelope going the right way, and he always seals it before checking its position. When we were married, I developed a system for paying bills with him. I would sit next to him and stuff the envelopes and apply the stamps. It helped Vince avoid a lot of meltdowns.

"I prefer writing out the checks. It's one of the last things I am able to do, and I don't want that taken away from me." He looks so sad and frail as he sits in the chair.

"I understand," I say.

"Are you doing okay financially? How is your business doing?"

"Honestly, things are tight. My business is struggling," I continue. "And before I moved in, we talked about you continuing to pay some portion of child support. You have yet to give me any money."

Vince had said he'd pay for everything, but he hasn't. Trying to get reimbursed for expenditures has proven difficult. I have to justify and explain every expense for Kate or the house, and Vince often admonishes me for a purchase. The constant money conversation drains me. Vince even scrutinizes the grocery bill and chastises me for buying food at certain stores.

One rainy afternoon, I took the kids to the bookstore to look at books and magazines. Of course, I love that they continue to enjoy reading, so I purchased several books and magazines for them both. I even called Vince to see if he would like us to pick up any new reading material for him. Once home, I placed the bill for $85 on his desk so he could reimburse me. Later that night, he told me that trips to the bookstore are not essential and that he will not reimburse me for these kinds of expenses.

I continue paying bills online while Vince looks at me.

"I really appreciate what you have done for me, Karen. I see how hard you are working to build your company and I am so proud of you for making something of yourself after our divorce. I hear you on the telephone, and you really understand sales and marketing. You are a great sales person."

I look up. I do appreciate his kind words. Vince has never been one to compliment me.

"You know, you will get some insurance money when I pass." he reminds me. Per our divorce decree, we are both responsible for maintaining a designated amount of insurance until the youngest child turns 18 years old. This money is to be used to help care for the children if either one of us should die.

"I know," I say. Unfortunately, this does not help my current cash-flow situation.

"Is there something else I can do to make things easier for you and the kids," he asks.

I take a deep breath. I am not sure what his plans are for his house, but I am concerned about moving James and Kate again right after his death.

"I really don't want to move the kids again after you are gone. They will be dealing with so much. Moving again will be stressful for us all. I would like them to be able to come home from college to their home, your home."

"Do you like living here?" Vince asks with surprise.

"Yes, I do. It's such a beautiful home, and your neighbors are all so wonderful."

"Why don't you stay in the house as long as you want?" he says. "You just pay the utilities and homeowner's association dues. The trust will take care of the mortgage, insurance and anything else. Will that give you some breathing room?"

I could hardly believe what he was saying.

"Yes. That would be great!" My eyes fill with tears. He has just given me the best gift, some breathing room.

In the coming months as he becomes sicker, I will not be plagued with worry about missed billable hours and time away from my company. I am comforted knowing that I will not have to move the kids again. The last move was so traumatic that I have blocked any recollection of packing the house or moving, much like when a woman gives birth. I just want time to catch my breath after he passes. I want the children to have time to grieve before life has to change again.

I am overwhelmed with gratitude. His generosity is completely out of character, but I assume his terminal diagnosis has made him realize what is really important. This bold act is so out of place that I convince myself that he means what he is saying.

Vince's act of kindness allows me to delude myself into believing I have forgiven him. How can I hold a grudge or ill feelings against Vince, in light of this act of kindness?

Maybe Vince is beginning to soften and see all the love that is around him. Maybe he sees all that the children and I are sacrificing to live with him and he wants to make things easier for us after he passes. I have always theorized that it is never too late to change or reinvent yourself.

***

April 27, 2012

I wake up this morning filled with relief. The sun is shining, and I feel like the weight of the world has been lifted from my shoulders. Vince has promised to let me stay in the house with the kids for as long as I want. I have been working long hours at night trying to keep myself afloat financially. Now, at least I will not have to worry about where the kids and I will live after Vince is gone. I will have a home and some breathing space to get back on my feet. This gift will allow me to focus on the kids and help them get through grieving for Vince. I smile to myself. Vince finally understands what is important. It is too bad that it has taken this tragedy to make Vince a softer person. I am filled with gratitude.

CHAPTER SEVEN

MAY — BAD NEWS

I am traveling to Detroit, Michigan, for a conference with my business partner. This is one of the most important conferences each year for one of my customers. I have participated the last three years, and even though Vince is sick, it is critical that I attend this year. The conference is an opportunity for us to market our customer and create visibility for our own company. I will only be away for two nights and I am looking forward to the separation.

Vince is meeting with his Chicago oncologist to get the results from his last PET scan today. The last time we met with him, Vince was not feeling well and was concerned more tumors were growing. He was also having a tremendous amount of trouble swallowing food. The time has arrived to discuss having a stint surgically implanted in his esophagus so he can continue to eat.

The drive to Detroit takes six hours. I keep checking my phone every few minutes for a call from Vince. I am nervous about what the doctor will say. My gut is in knots. I am afraid the news will be bad.

We decide to pull over for lunch, and just as we are ready to give our order to the waiter my phone rings. I jump up and tell my business partner to order me whatever she is having, and quickly make my way to the front lobby area of the restaurant.

"Hi, Vince."

"It's not good Karen. It's really, really bad."

I can hear the anguish in his voice, and my eyes fill with tears. In this moment, I am flooded with compassion for Vince. No one should die so young of such a horrible disease.

"I have 90 days," he says.

I immediately feel sick, and my stomach twists into tighter knots.

"What exactly did he say?"

He starts to sob. "The tumors have grown a lot. There is one on my hip. It's probably causing my leg pain. I asked the doctor how much time, and he said that if I make it to Labor Day, it will be a blessing. I don't know what to do."

I am so sad for James, Kate and Vince.

"We need to embrace everyday and enjoy it as much as we can," I say. "What did he say about the stint?"

I can barely understand his next sentence through his sobs. "I am seeing a surgeon tomorrow whose specialty is esophageal stints."

"Vince, I am so very sorry. I know this is not what you were expecting to hear. I'm sorry I am not there, but I will be with you every step of the way. We will make the best of it."

"I'll talk to you later," he says.

I head back to the table. My expression gives away the news. The horror of the situation engulfs me like an oversized dark cloak. This is the beginning of what will be the hardest part of our journey. Each day going forward, Vince will wake up with the knowledge that today is the best he will feel, and that tomorrow he will feel worse. It is time to reach out to hospice and begin to make plans. I can barely stand up with the enormity of it all bearing down on me.

As a take a breath I feel that sharp pain again in my chest. Ninety days to help care for Vince and help him die. Ninety days to facilitate healing between Vince and James. Ninety days for Kate to come to terms with losing her father. I am consumed with grief, anxiety and fear.

It is typical of caregivers in this situation to put all their focus and energy into everyone around them. I am no different. I have always put my family's needs ahead of my own needs.

As we continue the drive to Detroit, my thoughts drift to what lies ahead for my family. The grief is really overwhelming, and I am having trouble reconciling my feelings. How can I be filled with such grief for someone who treated me so callously in the past? I begin to realize, yet again, I have not forgiven Vince. Unfortunately, I am expending so much energy on everyone else that I have nothing left.

***

Vince meets with the surgeon the following day, and the doctor agrees to perform the surgery the next week. He will embed a stint in Vince's esophagus that will run the length of his tumor. This will allow him to eat regular foods. Vince is adamant that he does not want a feeding tube, so hopefully this will help him continue to eat and stay nourished.

***

On Tuesday, we make our way to the hospital for Vince's surgery. Vince can barely walk now, so I decide to drop him at the front doors. I circle around the building and drive up several levels in the parking garage until I find a spot. I make my way into the building and navigate a maze of hallways to find the Gastrointestinal Surgery Center. It has been about 15 minutes since I left Vince. As I round the corner to the waiting area, the elevator doors open and Vince shuffles off. I am shocked that he has just arrived. His inability to walk is deteriorating more and more each day.

He checks in with the wrong registration desk and is sent across the room. More walking. He grows agitated. Recently he has begun experiencing some confusion, and his thoughts get muddled easily. I suggest he sit down and let me check him in.

Unfortunately, even though Vince registered over the phone, we have to register once again. Vince is very frustrated at this point, so I walk with him to the registrar's cubicle. I answer most of the questions and occasionally I have to prompt Vince to answer. At one point I am cued to provide a copy of Vince's healthcare instructions (his DNR) and my power of attorney to make healthcare decisions. Suddenly, I am overwhelmed with sadness. If something goes wrong today, I will be the one making decisions about his care. I am apprehensive. I underestimated what a daunting responsibility this would be.

I try to stay positive for Vince. I'm sure he is nervous enough about the surgery. As with any surgery, there are potential complications. His tumors could rupture, and he could bleed out.

The nurse provides a gown for Vince to change into, and I step out of the room. The nurse tells me that it's all right for me to stay, but I explain to her that I am Vince's ex-wife and that I'm sure he would prefer his privacy. It takes Vince a long while to undress. He is unsteady and has very little energy. I step back into the room and bag all his clothes and belongings. The nurse reminds him that he must remove all his jewelry including his necklace. He looks at me helplessly. He does not want to remove his Blessed Mother medallion, which he always wears. He never takes it off. I assure him that he will still be protected during surgery. I place her in a safe pocket inside my purse.

Vince's surgery is the last operation of the day, and the doctor is running behind. Gripped with worry, neither of us can speak. We try to make idle conversation but we are both nervous. Finally, the anesthesiologist arrives and speaks with us. He confirms again that there will be no life-saving measures. Vince must answer a list of questions. He nods his head in agreement to each one. I am uncomfortable, and guilt pervades my thoughts. I feel guilty that I will go on living, and Vince will be stripped of that opportunity. I am painfully aware that I will get to see James and Kate finish maturing, that I will get to witness all of their amazing milestones along the way, but that Vince will not. Why do those of us who go on living feel so guilty?

The nurse arrives. It is time for surgery. I stand and awkwardly squeeze Vince's hand. I am no longer his wife, but I am his caretaker now. The responsibility is burdensome. I place my other hand on his very skinny arm. His arms and legs have shrunk in the last few weeks. He barely has any muscle left. The cancer is eating his body.

"I will see you when you wake up," I say.

"See you, and thank you." A tear slowly runs down his cheek. I know he is scared he won't survive the surgery. I am concerned, too, but somehow I know that this is not the end.

I smile comfortingly and look him in the eye. "I will see you when you wake up." I tilt my head to one side, asking for confirmation from him that he understands. He nods his head *yes* and forces a weak smile. I watch as the nurse wheels him away through the doors.

I head to the waiting room and watch the monitor for his name. The procedure takes a little more than an hour, but another 30 minutes pass before he wakes up in recovery.

I try to keep myself busy answering emails and working on marketing projects. It is impossible to focus. I keep looking to the monitor every few minutes and anxiously glancing to the door each time a surgeon arrives in the waiting room to collect a family. Finally, Vince's name appears on the monitor, and a nurse summons me to the recovery area.

Vince is sitting up and coughing uncontrollably. He holds a pink trough in front of his mouth. He looks exhausted and bleary from the anesthesia. I wonder how I will put him in the car and how he will climb the stairs at home. The nurse has brought in some apple juice for him to sip. He has not eaten all day. I hold the apple juice bottle and a straw. His expression is that of a little boy, and I giggle as he chases the straw trying to get it into his mouth.

He smiles. "I love apple juice."

In these moments of vulnerability, I feel only compassion and empathy for Vince.

He will be on a clear liquid diet for the night and then soft foods beginning tomorrow. The surgeon comes by to explain the procedure. He has implanted the longest stint available into Vince's esophagus. Unfortunately, the tumor is longer than the stint, so the surgeon had to strategically place the stint so that it holds open as much of the tumor as possible. Vince's cancer began with a tumor in his stomach that has grown up his esophagus. The tumor in his stomach is located on the right side, so the surgeon has placed the stint reaching into the left side.

Vince asks how long the stint will keep his esophagus open?

The doctor pauses. "Until the end," he says.

His words hang in the air like a noose waiting to hang a prisoner.

The surgeon's physician assistant comes by with discharge papers and eating instructions. Vince is still very groggy from his sedation. I stand next to the PA looking at the discharge notes. She instructs me that Vince will need to stay away from fruits and vegetables with skins because they may lodge in his stint. The stint is a mesh coil that can easily become impacted, so patients have to follow a careful diet. If food lodges in the coil, it will have to be surgically removed. This puts the tumor at risk for tearing and bleeding. Vince could then bleed out. It is imperative he follow the diet that has been laid out.

I ask if cherries are on the no-no list. She nods her head yes.

Recently, Vince has been consuming a bag of cherries every night.

"No more cherries, big guy," I say, trying to lighten the mood.

He looks up at me with an innocent boy-like expression. "No cherries?" He frowns and adds, "But I love my cherries."

"I know," I say.

Vince's normally gruff attitude is clouded by his grogginess, and I can't help but smile at his expressions of innocence. "We'll get you some cherry ice-cream. It will taste just as good and make your throat feel better."

He frowns again with a look of consternation. "But I really love my cherries."

I pat his hand. "I know. We will work it out. It will be okay."

The nurse comes in and hands me Vince's clothes.

"Can you help him get dressed, or do you need me to do it?" she asks.

"I can help him," I say.

This is the first time that I have needed to help Vince dress. He can barely lift his legs to put his shorts on. I slip his feet into his shoes and tie them. I had tried to encourage him to wear his flip-flops so he could just slide them on after surgery, but he insisted on wearing his sneakers.

There are moments I just want to scream, "Please just do it my way, because it will be easier for me." Everything is a negotiation. I suspect Vince feels like he is losing control of his life, so he tries to dominate every situation. It's maddening. I do all the driving when we are together, but recently he has begun telling me how to drive. He tells me where to turn, which parking spot to take, which lane to be in—as if I have never driven before. Fortunately for Vince, I am a patient woman and just bite my tongue.

A volunteer arrives and helps him into a wheelchair. I pull the car around from the parking garage while an elderly gentleman wheels Vince down to the front door of the hospital. I help him into the car, and we head home.

Once we arrive home, James helps him inside the house and up the stairs to his bed.

That night as I drift off to sleep, I am filled with gratitude that the surgery was a success.

***

I spend the next day working from home so I can make sure Vince eats soft foods and consumes enough protein and calories. He is having a tremendous amount of chest pain, an unfortunate side effect of the stint. After insertion, the patient's natural body temperature warms the coil and it expands in his esophagus. Vince is miserable and now feels constant pressure and pain.

He also has to sleep semi-prone so the acid from his stomach will not travel up his esophagus. The pain initially causes him to regret having the surgery. He had no idea that he would have so much discomfort. We are quickly learning that everything has a trade off. The upside is that he will be able to eat food normally, but he will have chronic discomfort in his chest.

The pain takes a toll on him. He is absolutely exhausted. He has been in bed all day and evening and has barely eaten. I beg him to drink a protein shake, but he refuses.

Our palliative care nurse comes by to check on Vince. She tries to convince him to take additional pain medication in the form of morphine. At this point, Vince is on a 75-milligram pain patch and takes some additional oral pain medication each afternoon. The nurse explains how important it is to break the cycle of distress so his body can rest. He assures her that he will take something when needed.

I have had the medication conversation with Vince on many occasions, but he refuses to listen. Even now that the hospice nurse is encouraging him to manage his pain, he still resists. I am irritated that he refuses to listen to people who only have his best interest in mind. If he remains in a constant state of discomfort, he compromises his immune system and becomes irritable and explosive.

***

I have to fly to California for my uncle's memorial service. He died a month ago after battling throat cancer for more than two years. He was originally given six months to live, but he valiantly fought to buy more time. In the end his body just gave out, just like Vince's body will do. My uncle is in a better place now and hopefully pain free. I have just finished packing and head to Vince's room to check on him. I can't help but think that within the next few months I will be organizing Vince's memorial services and funerals.

I go to check on Vince before going to bed. I have an early flight to catch. Vince is lying slightly prone, and the room is dark. I carefully sit on the edge of the mattress and ask if there is anything I can do for him. I am uneasy about leaving him. He takes my hand and begins to talk.

"I can't go on like this," he says. "I am in so much pain. I simply don't have the strength to go on. I'm exhausted and I am tired of fighting. I'm going to try to hang on until you get back."

"What are you talking about?" I ask. "Are you feeling that bad?"

"I want to see my family one last time," says Vince, referring to their upcoming visit, which will take place while I am away.

"I will try to hold on until you get back," he says again. "Please come right home from the airport Monday. I don't want Kate to find me."

"What do you mean?" I ask, but I know deep in my gut that he is talking about taking his life.

"I mean, Monday morning after Kate leaves for school, I'm going to go to sleep and not wake up," he says.

"Vince, please don't do anything crazy. We can keep your pain under control with morphine."

"I've tried taking it, but it makes me feel like I'm choking."

"Listen, you can't do that while the kids are in the house. Please think about what you are doing and what you will put everyone through if you take your life."

"I can't do this anymore. I can't live my life like this in constant pain. I will wait for James to go to work and Kate to go to school. Just make sure you come home right away on Monday."

When Vince makes up his mind about something, it is impossible to dissuade him. I feel empty inside. Once again, I feel like I am negotiating with a child. I lie awake all night strategizing how to handle the situation. I am angry that he has saddled me with this information right before I am leaving. His family is arriving tomorrow afternoon to celebrate his birthday, and I know he will not do anything rash while they are here. Vince can also be overdramatic, and I am hoping this is one of those performances.

I am furious that he is ruining my trip to California and impacting my visit with my family. This is my time to grieve with them. How dare he make such a terrible threat? I almost feel like he is trying to manipulate me so that I will cancel my trip. Honestly, I would, if his family was not going to spend the weekend with him. His selfishness brings up all the memories of other times where he ruined evenings or vacations with his drama. Once more, I am confronted with the knowledge that I have not yet forgiven him.

***

As the taxi pulls away from the house the next morning to head to the airport, I break down. The enormity and stress that Vince's proclamation has put on me is more than I can bear. I look back at the house and contemplate asking the driver to turn around. I resolve to check in frequently with Vince and the kids and to fly home a day early so that I will arrive back before Monday.

I reluctantly board the plane. I am so worried about James and Kate. When I share the story with my mother, she is not surprised at his continued selfish behavior. I spend my entire trip texting Kate and checking in with Vince by telephone. I am sick with worry about what he is planning for Monday.

Vince's mother, brother, sister-in-law and nephew arrive on Vince's 54th birthday. I have asked Vince's mother to come care for him while I am in California. I am thankful that she will be with Vince to make sure he follows his diet restrictions. I even write a list of instructions for her on the blackboard in the kitchen in case she forgets anything we discussed over the phone. He is to have only soft foods for the next few days, no bread and no fruits and vegetables with skins. She assures me that she will take care of feeding him and even go grocery shopping once she gets in. I am indebted to her for her help. It is increasingly difficult to juggle taking care of Vince, his doctor's appointments, working full-time and keeping teens on track.

Later that weekend Kate texts me a photo of all the cakes, pastries and breads that have been purchased at the bakery. I am horrified. Vince is under strict orders to avoid these types of sticky foods.

Kate tells me how upset she is with Vince. She tries to remind him that he should not be eating muffins and bread, but he does so anyway. What Vince's ego fails to see is that every choice he makes impacts either his children or me. Kate cannot fathom why her father is not following the doctor's instructions.

I am worried what Monday will hold. My entire family still lives in California. Despite the unfortunate circumstances regarding my uncle's death, I was hoping to spend some quality time with them. Instead, Vince's threat distracts me.

I talk to my mother about my concerns. She is my best friend, and I value her opinion and insights. Sometimes you need the people around you to turn the mirror so you can clearly see your reflection. My mother is a pro at doing this. She has pointed out that, while I think I have forgiven Vince, I have not. She can still hear the anger and hurt in my voice when I talk about him. Of course, I am angry with him for threatening to take his life. But I truly believe I have forgiven him and I grow very annoyed with my mother's observation.

"I have forgiven Vince. How else could I have moved in with him?" I say.

"Have you really?" she asks.

I am suddenly aware of the fact that I have not forgiven him. I have been lying to everyone and sometimes to myself.

Deep inside, I still remember all the scary moments during our contentious divorce and all the hurtful words during our marriage. My emotional wounds have not healed. I can still recall how scared, powerless and abandoned I felt. I've been tricking myself into believing that if I just say the words, "I forgive him," everyday, eventually it will be true.

Actually, saying, "I forgive you," is just the first step and, honestly, the easiest step of all. In order to genuinely forgive, you must live it with your actions. I have been fooling myself by saying the words everyday and assuming that just because I chose to move in and care for him that I have forgiven.

I am so disappointed in myself. I have not been living authentically. I am so tired of feeling hate. I am aware that the anger and animosity are consuming me and stealing my energy. Vince's threat to take his life has pushed me to the edge. I can no longer keep the negative emotions and memories contained in the box. If I don't address forgiving, I will miss the opportunity to create peace and closure between us. My own health and well-being are at stake.

***

I awake early the next morning with such a strong desire to find forgiveness. I yearn to rid my body and mind of all the resentment. I Google *forgiveness* on my laptop. Surely there is someone who has been through this before and has a proven process I can implement. I am discouraged by the information I find. Most of the articles I read focus on writing down the things that you need to forgive and tearing them up and replacing your thoughts with the words, "I forgive." It would take weeks to write down all the hurtful moments, and doing so would feel like taking a step back. I don't want to think about those moments anymore. I am not finding any useful advice. I decide to head out for a long run.

I set off on my run listening to a U2 playlist. A smile spreads across my face as I remember listening to this album in the first condo Vince and I shared. Those were happier, simpler times. Then memories of his hurtful words begin to invade my thoughts again.

I have an epiphany. In order to truly forgive Vince, I need to assume a new role in our relationship. I have always acted like a victim to Vince's rages, bad behavior and emotional abuse. I surrendered control with each tantrum when I chose not to stand up to him. I need to forgive myself for each time I chose to keep quiet. I also need to accept the fact that my love for Vince was not enough to change him. How Vince chooses to behave is his path or journey, and how I react is mine. I have had choices all along. I just didn't exercise that right. I am a strong, independent woman, and it is time I act that way with Vince.

The second step in forgiving Vince is to forgive myself for playing a victim and for my own actions in our marriage. I can't begin to forgive Vince until I forgive myself. I was 23 when we married, and I realize that my immaturity and lack of experience made it difficult to create a stable relationship. I didn't have the skills to cope with Vince, and I was naïve enough to believe that he would change. I am aware that Vince must have lacked the skills to be married, as well. His ego was so large that it dominated everything around it, including me. If I forgive myself for being immature, then I can forgive Vince for his lack of experience, too. I head back to Chicago determined to find a way to forgive before it is too late.

***

Through phone calls, I've learned that Vince's chest pain seems to be diminishing. The physical drain of the constant discomfort is gone. By the end of the weekend his spirits are high, once again, and thoughts of ending his life have been pushed out of his consciousness.

I fly home and arrive to find Vince in a great mood. He is almost euphoric and can't stop talking about what a great weekend he had with his family. There is absolutely no mention of his previous threat of eternal sleep. I am angry with myself for buying into the drama and for allowing it to impact my weekend.

**

Memorial Day weekend arrives, and Vince's three best friends fly in to visit. He has known them since college. One of them will be the trustee for the children's estate. Vince is not feeling well, and his energy is low, but he is determined to see one last Cubs game. He has been planning this visit with the guys for a while. We don't have the proper space to accommodate so many guests, so his friends stay at a local hotel. It's been a long time since I have seen them, and I am looking forward to reconnecting.

It's a great weekend filled with lots of stories and laughs. Vince manages to stay up most days until eight or nine at night. He is willing his body to cooperate. He no longer has pain in his esophagus. He soaks up every minute of time with his friends because he is not sure when he will see them again. I plan a Memorial Day barbecue with some of Vince's favorite foods that are within his diet. I encourage James and Kate to invite some friends to come by for dinner, as well. It's a full house. Vince is visibly happy as he sits at the head of the dining room table surveying the swarm of activity and lively conversations. He smiles, and I am thrilled that the kids have included their friends. This is exactly what I had envisioned when I suggested we all live together. Life feels very good at this moment.

**

On the last day the guys are in town, Vince and I sit down with the trustee for Vince's estate. The trust is designed to support the children while they are students. The trustee and I will work together to decide appropriate disbursements as the kids head off to college. Vince begins to read through the trust agreement. The beginning of the trust is straightforward and outlines his healthcare power of attorney. I will be responsible for making those decisions. Everyone turns the page to the next set of documents, and all at once tears spring to my eyes. I am shocked to see that the trust stipulates that the children and I will be allowed to live in Vince's house for two years as long as I pay rent and all associated expenses. Vince continues blissfully reading along unaware that I am upset. The trust further stipulates that at the end of two years the trust will sell the house. I am so hurt that I cannot speak. Tears continue to fill my eyes, and I know at any minute the floodgates will open. Adrenaline races through my body. *Why did he go back on his word?* Previously, he had agreed to allow the children and I to live in the house indefinitely. The bottom line is that once the children stop coming home from college, I will want to move on. But until then, I want continuity for them. They have been through so much, divorce and now the eventual loss of their father. I feel as if I have been kicked in the stomach. My heart is shattered, and my world has just crashed in around me. I am trying very hard not to cry. I can't read anything through the pool of tears. I've stopped listening to Vince as he continues reading. I can no longer sit at the table. I slowly stand.

"This is not what we discussed," I say.

I am devastated. I have given up so much so he can have time with his children. I have put my personal life on hold and spent countless hours away from work. Clearly, my sacrifices mean nothing to this man. After all I have done and all I will sacrifice, this is what he feels is appropriate. What happened to our conversation last month about wanting to make things easier for the kids and me after he passes? What happened to the breathing room he promised?

I feel hopeless. He has not changed at all. He still does not understand what is really important. Time and family are priceless gifts, and I have given him both.

Money continues to be the center of Vince's universe. I know he is angry that he has worked so hard to amass a substantial nest egg that he will never have the luxury of spending. Vince has the opportunity to make life less stressful for the children and me. He could provide financial comfort. Apparently, I am not worthy of this comfort, and I feel abandoned all over again.

I can't listen to anymore. Tears stream down my face as I leave the house. I feel like such a fool. I trusted him to follow through with his promises. I have not taken a single dollar from him during my stay. Before we moved in, he promised to take care of all of our expenses. I have spent thousands of dollars moving in and paying for a storage unit for my belongings because they don't fit in his home. I feel so disrespected. My priceless gift is worthless to Vince.

I walk up and down the street trying to compose myself. I am so agitated, I feel like I might jump out of my skin. I call my mother and share with her what has just happened. I can barely speak the words through the deep sobs from my heart.

"You need to move out," she says. "You did not sign up to take care of him and put yourself at financial risk. I was afraid he would take advantage of you!"

I think for several minutes as she continues talking. My thoughts drift to James and Kate, the entire reason I moved in to Vince's home.

"Mom, I can't move out. What kind of message would that send to James and Kate? It makes it seem like it's all about the money. What would they think of Vince? I don't want them to think badly of their father."

Even at this moment, I am protecting Vince's reputation with his children.

"I moved in so they could mend their relationship with him. If I move out, it will destroy their relationship. I can't do that to them."

"So you understand that you are putting yourself at financial risk?"

I can hear the disappointment in her voice.

I have no choice but to stay. I am committed to helping James and Kate make peace with their father. If I move out, this will shine a spotlight on Vince's failings, and I refuse to do that to the children. They only have a few months to soak up time with him. We have just months left to live together as a family. I cling to the notion that staying is the right thing to do.

"I will make it work," I say. "What can I do now? I can't move out. It would destroy the kids."

I take a long walk and stay outside for quite a while. I am struggling with my emotions. Even though months earlier I was ready to move out, this is different. In March, it was the children that were asking to move out. This move would be because of me and it would be selfish. When I come back inside, Vince looks visibly worried. I am so hurt that I cannot look him in the eyes.

"Karen, talk to me. I'll take care of this." He stands in front of me, but I cannot look him in the eyes. I try to walk around him, but he blocks me. He knows just how upset I am. It's never a good sign when I refrain from talking.

"I promise to take care of this. Karen, please I need you. I promise to fix things."

He knows exactly what is wrong. He knows he has lied to me.

"I'll call the attorney tomorrow and have him draft a document that says you and the kids can stay as long as you want in the house."

Once again I attempt to walk away without looking at him. He shifts his entire body in front of me again, and this time puts his hands on my arms to stop me.

"Karen, please I will take care of this. Don't worry."

How am I ever going to find forgiveness when he continues to disrespect my gift?

May 28, 2012

I am so exhausted and so tired of feeling this way. I know deep in my heart that I am doing the right thing for James and Kate. I just wish Vince would step up and be the man I know he can be. I wish he would just think with his heart now. It's over. He will die in just a few months, and I wish he could put his family first. I am sad that he may die and not ever understand how blessed he was to have James, Kate and I with him at the end. I am so exhausted. As I drift to sleep, I pray for a plan to forgive. I need to forgive.

CHAPTER EIGHT

JUNE — FORGIVENESS

June arrives bursting with the promise of new beginnings. Kate finishes her junior year, and James is preparing to leave for college in August.

We have begun a sophisticated dance in our home of discussing plans for the future. We are always aware that Vince may not be here.

Vince becomes increasingly weaker, and he spends most of his time sleeping. He is able to rally some energy each day for a late lunch. He is in constant pain and can barely walk. I am overwhelmed helping him manage his pain and expectations. He vacillates between sadness and anger. He has trouble accepting what the cancer is doing to his body.

Last month, I persuaded Vince to begin interviewing hospice agencies to ready ourselves for the inevitable. Most people do not realize that during a serious illness many hospice facilities offer palliative care. Certified nurses work directly with the family in the home, managing pain and symptoms. A nurse visits once a week and orders all the medications and any equipment needed to care for the terminally ill patient. We also have 24/7 access to an on-call nurse should we have any questions regarding how to manage Vince's symptoms. I recommend finding a hospice facility early on, especially if your goal is to have your family member die at home.

In addition, to setting up hospice care, Vince wants to make sure all the funeral arrangements are selected and paid for in advance. He asks me to schedule a meeting to visit the local funeral home. I feel very awkward making these arrangements together, but I appreciate that Vince is attempting to lessen the burden on me after he passes. We drive to the funeral home together while Vince talks about his vision for the two memorial services that he expects to have. One will be held in Chicago and the other in Pennsylvania, where he was born and his family still resides. The funeral director is surprised to have Vince participate in the planning of his own services. Frankly, I am very uncomfortable with the situation, as well, but Vince insists.

Vince has spoken with the children about his wish to be cremated. His ashes will be given to the children. The children will have the opportunity to scatter his ashes at a location of their choosing. However, the Catholic religion's practice is that cremains must be buried in a consecrated grave in a Catholic cemetery. We want to honor Vince's mother and his Catholic upbringing. We explain this to the funeral director, and she suggests that the remains be split in half with Vince's mother receiving one half and James and Kate receiving the other half. She also suggests splitting the portion designated to the children into thirds. Each child would receive a third of Vince's remains sealed in an urn. A third of the ashes would then be designated for the children to spread. The children's urns would never need to be opened.

The funeral director escorts us to a separate room where urns and keepsake boxes for cremains are displayed. We are both ill at ease in front of the display case. Tears pool in my eyes, and I cannot see the urns. I am afraid to look at Vince. I bite my lower lip hard, trying to hold back the tears. The enormity of the situation is more than I can handle.

I take a deep breath. "Did you have something in mind?" I ask.

Vince has tears in eyes, as well. This is absolutely more than either of us is ready to handle. "Can you just choose something?"

"Absolutely," I smile weakly and turn to the director. "Can I get back to you on the urns?"

She nods in agreement and quickly adds, "I think it is so wonderful of you to make these arrangements ahead of time so your wife will not be burdened with the responsibility."

Vince looks at me playfully and smiles wide. "She's my ex-wife."

The funeral director looks at me then at Vince. She is at a loss for words.

"Can we go?" Vince urges.

"Of course."

We head towards the stairs.

"Please prepare all the paperwork. I will come by next week to pay for everything," Vince says.

The funeral director offers to come to our home instead. She can see the pain and grief that surrounds us.

I will not let her come to the house to sign final papers until Vince has finally passed. While I understand Vince's need to control even his funeral, it is too dispiriting to plan your own memorial services. Perhaps I shouldn't care anymore about his need for control. Yet it irks me. At the same time, I am tired of living with feelings of hate. It takes so much energy to hate him, and it exhausts me. I struggle to embrace living in a state of grace, no matter what Vince chooses to do. I realize that this is the next step in forgiveness, living in a state of grace. I am doing what is right and I need to remember that.

I feel a shift today. I no longer view Vince as my ex-husband, but as a man who is dying and deserves to be cared for as a human being. It is heartbreaking to watch him get sicker by the day. I am resolved to providing care and comfort to him so he can have as much time as possible with

James and Kate. My actions will become an integral part of the forgiveness process. It is easy to say the word *forgiveness*, but the challenge is to live in forgiveness.

***

Kate and I travel to Philadelphia in mid June. She is having an elective surgery, and we are both staying at Vince's mother's home. James has to work, but he is able to care for Vince during his down time. James calls one afternoon to tell me Vince is choking on a beef sandwich. He refuses to let the cancer dictate what he can and cannot eat. He takes a stand against the cancer by eating what he wants when he wants. It's the second time he has tried to eat an Italian beef sandwich only to have it get stuck in his stint. His refusal to follow the doctor's instructions regarding the type of foods he should eat is exasperating. His destructive behavior places a tremendous amount of pressure on James, Kate and myself. The surgeon has warned him that if something gets stuck, they will have to remove the stint, which stretches the length of his tumor. Removing the stint could puncture his tumor and he could bleed out.

I am a mix of emotions. I am angry with Vince for being so thoughtless. I sympathize with James and understand how scared he must be.

"Dad told me that if he can't clear his throat, I will have to drive him to the emergency room."

I can hear the fear in James' voice.

"That's ridiculous. Call 911. Hang up now and call."

I am furious with Vince. Eventually, Vince is able to clear his throat and does not need to go to the hospital. James now turns his frustration on me for leaving him home alone with his father. He sends a barrage of texts.

"It was a bad idea for you and Kate to be gone at the same time. How could you leave me home alone with Dad? He isn't feeling well and he says he is in a ton of pain. You need to come home."

James has no place to direct his anger. He knows his relationship with is father is too fragile for a confrontation. Instead, he takes his frustration out on me.

***

Vince is flying in this morning to Philadelphia. He has organized a "reunion" weekend with all his business associates in Baltimore. He is supposed to arrive this afternoon. Tomorrow morning we will drive two hours south to Baltimore to meet up with everyone.

I am awakened by his early morning call.

"I can't walk," he says through sobs. "How can I fly today?"

My stomach twists in knots. We have dreaded this point when Vince might become bedridden. We always knew this might be a possibility. With each day the end grows nearer. The cancer is stealing him away bit by bit. I sit in the chair hugging my knees to my chest.

"Everyone is coming in for this weekend," he says. "How can I cancel? Everyone was looking forward to seeing me."

"Vince," I say, "everyone knows you have cancer. We told everyone there might be a possibility that you would be too weak to travel."

"I know, but I told everyone last week that this weekend was a go and I would definitely be there."

He is inconsolable.

"Everyone will understand. You have had a setback and there is nothing we can do about it. You are unable to travel, and everyone will understand. I'll let James know he needs to help you today, and I will call everyone else. I will be on the first flight out tomorrow morning back to Chicago. I'll call you once I have finished alerting everyone and have changed my flight. Just try to go back to sleep. Maybe take some morphine for your pain."

"Okay. I can't wait for you to get home." His voice is filled with pain and anxiety.

I feel beaten. The cancer is winning. Later in the morning, I explain to Vince's mother what is happening.

"Is it time?" she asks. She wants to know when she should make her way to Chicago to see her son for the last time.

There is no way for me to know when it's time. Right now, I'm just focused on what needs to be done at home and supporting James and Kate. Everyone wants to know when to come. Regrettably, I don't have a crystal ball. I just don't know and the question feels like such a burden.

I realize she is looking for me to tell her what to do. She is frozen in her own grief with the knowledge that her son is dying. I am beginning to feel resentful that Vince's family is not more involved in his care and in supporting the children. I moved in so Vince could spend quality time with his children, but I expected his family would visit more frequently and provide support for the kids and me. While they all visited for Vince's birthday, I had expected his mother would visit as much as possible so she could spend time with Vince and connect with her grandchildren.

Vince's health is declining, and no matter how many rosaries his mother says, there will not be a miracle. Labor Day is quickly approaching. I encourage Vince's mother to fly to Chicago with Kate the following week. "I think you need to visit Vince now. I don't know when things will take a turn for the worse," I say.

***

I am home the next morning before Vince is even awake. I set to work walking the dog, cleaning the kitchen, doing laundry and grocery shopping. Vince wakes around noon, and I am able to convince him to have a protein drink. He then decides to shower.

Showers are a mini battle for Vince. I have removed all the rugs from the tile floor so he will not slip. Thankfully, his shower has a tile bench so he can sit. Washing and drying

93

himself requires every bit of energy he has. Showers last almost 45 minutes from start to finish, and then he must lie down for an hour or two to rebuild his strength. I check on him and spend the afternoon sitting next to him in his bed talking and reading. My heart is so heavy. It is so difficult to see him so helpless. I remember how physically strong he once was.

Next week he will begin a round of radiation to attempt to shrink the tumors on his spine that are impacting his ability to walk. Hopefully, this will provide some relief from the chronic pain.

***

June 24, 2012

> *Today I awake with a burning need to forgive Vince and to accept him for who he is. I still find myself judging and condemning him. I realize this is not forgiveness. I am so tired of hating, being sad and remembering all the hurtful moments. Time has not erased any of the hurt. Today I feel the exhaustion of all the years of unresolved feelings. I'm done thinking about these emotions. His actions, most recently with the house remind me of the past, and all the old emotions come bubbling up. Why can't I put his behavior in perspective? My anger has exhausted me, and I am desperate to forgive.*

I am reluctant to forgive Vince because he may look at forgiveness as reconciliation. I do not want a relationship with Vince. He broke my spirit more than a decade ago, and I never want to feel that pain again. I am afraid to forgive because I feel like it will lead to surrendering myself to Vince's ego. I am a bundle of conflicted emotions. I want to forgive, but I worry that it will lead to the loss of myself again. I am apprehensive that he will use my forgiveness to take advantage of me yet again.

I am empathetic to Vince's situation. But my empathy does not automatically translate to forgiveness. I fear that forgiving means surrendering.

I realize I must stop expecting Vince to be different. His ego will not allow him to change. I am aware that it is Vince's behavior that I dislike so much. If I separate him from his behavior, I can accept him for who he is, a human being. This is difficult for me because I believe we all have to own our actions. We choose our behavior.

I am desperate to stop feeling hurt and to forgive. This step is hard for me because I am surrendering my right to relive the past. I can no longer play the old videos. I have relinquished the past, but this does not mean I have to give up my power to Vince.

This is a pivotal moment. Vince is a human being, the father of our children and he deserves compassion, empathy and most of all, comfort. My body begins to feel a little lighter. I am empowered knowing that I have taken a giant leap towards forgiving Vince by separating him from his behavior.

An interesting outcome from this thought process is that I begin to feel better about myself. I feel a sense of relief and pride that I have found a way to stave off the negative memories.

I can hear that Vince is awake. I head to his room to help him take his morning medications and have a protein drink.

He sits on the side of his bed, and I sit across from him in a large wingback chair. I am filled with peace and light. I am focusing on no longer feeling resentment. I pour out the prescribed amount of medication from each container and hand the pills in pairs to Vince. He looks tired this morning, and I try to lift his spirits with talk of Kate's return and his mother's arrival. I place a straw in his protein drink and hand it to him with a smile.

"I really appreciate you flying home to take care of me." He looks up.

"Of course. I told you that we will get through this as a family. Why don't you get some more sleep?"

Upon reflection, I'm aware that my small gestures of handing him his medication and helping him drink some nourishment comforts Vince. I have the ability to demonstrate my concern for Vince through my actions.

I remember somewhere in the Bible a quote, "If your enemies are hungry, feed them." This will become the cornerstone of my forgiveness.

I have always had a passion for cooking. I love food, and cooking has always been a way for me to demonstrate my love for my family and friends. When Vince and I were married, we would entertain often. I always loved preparing gourmet meals that rivaled any four-star restaurant. I would spend hours reading cooking magazines, preparing menus, organizing grocery lists and, of course, cooking the meal. I enjoyed setting the table to create a mood for each occasion.

As a stay-at-home mom, I used to spend hours making almost everything we ate from scratch, including homemade breads, desserts, salad dressings and soups. I like to use healthy ingredients to layer flavors and create sumptuous meals.

I remember how much Vince enjoyed the food I used to prepare. After we divorced and I went back to work, I often did not have time to cook lavish gourmet meals. Today I decide that I will return to cooking. It's something that has always made Vince feel appreciated. I vow to rediscover my passion and use it to connect love with my actions. I will pour love into every meal I prepare, and it will begin tonight.

I will attach love to each and every thing I do to create a meal. I am aware that there is no way that I will ever love Vince again. However, I can focus my love on my cooking. If I pour passion into every aspect of the dish, then my appreciation will eventually carry through to Vince. Every movement will come from the love in my heart, and eventually, I will begin to emanate love naturally.

I carefully plan a menu that Vince will be able to swallow. It is a simple yet tasty dinner of mushroom risotto and caprese salad. I lovingly slice the heirloom tomatoes and fresh buffalo mozzarella. I alternate the slices of tomato and cheese in a circle on the plate. I drizzle green extra virgin olive oil and dark purple balsamic vinegar. I grind sea salt and black pepper onto the slices. Then I add the final touch, torn basil leaves. I am pleased with the presentation and smile as I turn my attention to the risotto.

I choose risotto because it requires 30 minutes to prepare and must be stirred continually. I carefully sauté minced sweet onions in a tablespoon of extra virgin olive oil. Once the onions are translucent, I add two cups of Arborio rice and stir until the rice is coated in olive oil. I carefully add one cup of Vouvray wine, one of Vince's favorites. I stir the rice continually until all the wine is absorbed. I add one-cup of chicken broth and add more broth in intervals to break down the starch in the rice and create the perfect consistency. With every addition of stock, I imagine pouring my love into the risotto. As I stir, I imagine breaking down the hurts and resentments from the past. I focus on the empathy I have for Vince. Preparing dinner tonight becomes a cathartic experience. I am filled with gratitude, grace and love. Peace washes over me.

Vince, James and I sit down to dinner, and Vince eats two helpings of risotto. This is the most I have seen him eat in a long while. He can't stop talking about how good it tastes and that it is the best risotto he has ever had. James even comments on how delicious the caprese salad is. There are no leftovers tonight. The boys have enjoyed every last bite. That night, Vince is less agitated and seems to be in a very content place. It is amazing how this simple gift of making a home-cooked meal can bring such positive, loving energy. Armed with this feedback, I decide to put love in everything I do from this day forward. With every fold of laundry, every push of the grocery cart, every stir of a pot and every word spoken, I will emanate love.

As I try to drift off to sleep, I am filled with peace and gratitude. Tonight was the beginning of my path towards forgiveness. Each time Vince's behavior brings up negative emotions, I must hit the stop button. His behaviors are separate from him as a human being. Everyone deserves compassion and empathy.

***

Today is James' 19th birthday. It was nineteen years ago at 3:45 p.m. (PST) that our little bundle of joy arrived, six pounds and 15 ounces. The births of both our children were the happiest days of our lives.

Today, Vince is heartbroken. He is consumed with anguish and the realization that today is the last time he will ever wish James a happy birthday. I cannot imagine how heartbroken he must be and the regret he must feel for all the birthdays he missed or took for granted. However, my concern turns to James. *I wonder how he must be feeling today? Has he realized this is his last birthday with his father?* He will never again hear his father say, "Happy Birthday."

***

Kate returns home and Vince's mother comes to visit. We are all heading downtown to have brunch with Vince's best friend and his wife. Last month, I instructed James and Kate that they were no longer allowed to ride in the car with Vince when he drives. The cocktail of pain medication he takes daily makes it difficult for him to concentrate, and I am concerned he may have an accident. Vince is incredulous when I share my concerns with him. I explain that all the pain medication could impair his driving ability and it would be tragic if he were in an accident and injured someone. He refuses to give up control of driving a car, so I alert him that the children are no longer allowed to ride with him. If he wants to go somewhere with James or Kate, then one of them must drive. I should call his doctor to discuss having his license suspended, but I feel it is not my place.

While having coffee with his mother before we leave, I share my concerns regarding Vince's driving. I explain that I will be driving downtown. She absolutely agrees, and I am grateful to have her support.

Vince calls out that it is time to leave. I yell down that I will be right there and I'll drive. A few minutes later, I head out the door to find Vince in the driver's seat, and his mother sitting in back. I approach the driver-side door and tell Vince that I am driving.

"No. I am. Get in," he says.

"Vince, you are taking too many pain pills to be driving. Let me drive."

"No. I'm fine. Just get in."

"Vince it's not safe. I won't risk getting into an accident. You're medicated, and it is hard to focus. I'm not endangering my life to go to brunch."

I look back at his mom for support.

"I didn't take any pain medication this morning," he argues back.

"He seems fine, Karen." Vince's mother says.

I am furious. We continue to square off in the driveway. The entire argument is about Vince and his control. I am angry that his mother gives in to him. I feel disrespected, and most of all, I feel like my life must be far less important than Vince's wishes. I am disgusted with both of them. I begrudgingly climb into the backseat doubting myself, wondering if I am making a bigger deal of this than is needed.

Vince erupts. "What the hell are you doing? Sit up front."

"If you are going to risk my life, then I want as much padding around me as possible. Maybe your mother would like to sit up front."

She quietly opens the door and moves to the passenger seat. I am silent the entire ride and all through brunch. I speak not a word to anyone. I'm not sure why I didn't refuse to go at all.

After brunch as we walk to the car, I say, "Give me the keys. I am driving."

Vince hands them over without a word. We drive home in silence. When we arrive home I ask Vince to stay in the driveway for a minute so I can speak with him.

"From now on," I say, "when we need to drive somewhere together, I will drive. It is irresponsible of you to risk our lives. Are you really willing to kill us both just so you can drive? Please think of James and Kate."

"You have no idea what it is like to have your life taken away from you," he says.

"You're right. I have no idea what it feels like to be you. I have no idea what it feels like to wake up each morning and know that I am dying. But you need to understand that I am afraid because I am all that James and Kate will have left. They will have lost you, and I can't let them lose their last parent."

"I can't give up driving yet," Vince says. "If I do, I will have nothing left. I can barely read anymore. It takes me all day just to read the newspaper. I can't eat my favorite foods. I need to be able to drive."

"Then you can drive alone. But neither the kids nor I will ride in the car with you at the wheel. I'm done talking about this." I turn and walk inside, ending our conversation.

Vince's ego continues to prioritize his life. Once again, the well-being of his children or anyone else is unimportant. It is more important for him to be able to drive. I feel sad for him. His ego will not allow him to care about anyone other than himself.

CHAPTER NINE

JULY — A BREAK

Last month's radiation of the spinal tumors was successful. The tumors have shrunk enough so that Vince no longer feels pain in his right leg. His hair has grown back, and he is now entirely grey. He is thin and shuffles like a 90-year-old man. His energy is waning, which makes climbing the stairs to his bedroom very difficult. He must slowly ascend one stair at a time. Most days his face takes on a light grey pallor, but every now and then he has a faint yellow hue. Could the tumor on his liver be responsible?

Vince still has an appetite. Unfortunately, he continues to eat the foods that connect him to his old life. I used to be filled with anger when he would insist on eating something that was on the "do-not-eat list." Now, I try to observe each situation as an outsider without all the emotion and memories of the past. This allows me to separate his actions from my feelings about him. The majority of the time, I understand his actions and what drives them: his ego, his need for control, his fear of dying. My new thought process leaves me feeling encouraged that I am making progress on my path to forgiveness.

Vince has always worked very hard to control every aspect of his life. He has never learned that the only thing we control as individuals is our reaction to the things that happen to us. By choosing to eat contraband food he attempts to assert control over the cancer. It's like flipping the middle finger to the disease.

I continue to use my passion for cooking as a conduit for my forgiveness. Food has always held an important place in Vince's life. When we were married, he often planned our vacations around the restaurants he wanted to dine at. I am gratified each day that I am preparing foods that Vince should eat and that the meals are healthy and delicious.

I had forgotten just how much I used to enjoy preparing meals for my family. I relish all the thought that goes into the meal, choosing unexpected ingredients and layering them together to create a tasty culinary treat. While I am using my cooking as a way to connect to Vince and demonstrate my forgiveness, it is also an escape. My thoughts and hands are focused on washing, chopping, dicing, sautéing and roasting. When I cook, I am able to forget that death is knocking at our door. This small gesture on my part makes all the difference in Vince's world. And I wake up most mornings filled with peace and serenity, knowing that I am helping to provide him with nourishment.

Today, I am preparing a tasty summer barbecue of brats soaked in beer and caramelized onions, gourmet beef burgers with bacon and blue cheese, summer corn salad, homemade potato salad, and dark chocolate brownies for dessert. Vince eats a burger without the bun so that it is easy to digest. I encourage Vince to invite his best friend and wife to join us. Having the house filled with people, laughter and good food gives everyone a break from the dark cloud that hangs over us.

***

Vince spends the majority of his time in bed these days. He tries to leave the house for an hour or two each day to eat lunch, buy a coffee or go to the bank. He continues to drive himself, an activity he refuses to give up.

He is so weak, though, he barely has the energy to walk around the house. Mornings are especially difficult. Energy eludes him, and sitting up in bed is an exhausting action. He now walks hunched over with the weight of his past and the fear of death strapped to his back. His left arm hangs, and he almost drags his left leg. The impact of the cancer is becoming more and more visible. We both can feel the end roaring towards us.

I have begun working from home. Vince requires an adult to be with him at all times in case he needs medication or help. Our mornings start very early. Vince usually wakes around 4 a.m. and needs his cocktail of pain medications, antacids and laxatives. He swallows about 12 pills each morning and it takes him quite a while to wash down all the meds. Once he is done with his medication, I sit with him while he eats a breakfast cracker and drinks an apple juice. I keep the conversation light. I share James' and Kate's schedules for the day. I never ask him how he is feeling. I know that each day he feels worse. He generally goes back to sleep, and I have about five or six hours before his day begins. I work out and manage to squeeze in half a day with my laptop before he wakes again.

Exercise has become as crucial to me as breathing. It is the only way that I can work out my stress and emotions. In my previous home, I had a full gym with a treadmill, elliptical machine, weights and a large area for yoga. When I moved to Vince's I was only able to bring one piece of equipment with me, the elliptical. It sits outside his room in the loft area. For the past six months, I have worked out for an hour each morning.

Recently I have begun to feel guilty for being able to work out. Vince will never be able to exercise again. I am conscious that the whirring sound of the elliptical may cause sadness and anger for him. So I have recently switched my routine. I sneak out each morning for a 30-minute run as soon as he goes back to sleep. I listen to several playlists, which help elicit the emotions I am trying to either purge or capture for the day. Often I am exhausted and just need some upbeat music to help me run faster and get my adrenaline pumping. On these days, I start each morning by walking the first few minutes and listening to *Amazing* by One Eskimo. This song connects me to my spiritual side. I am aware that nothing will ever be the same after Vince passes. This journey will profoundly change my life. Sometimes I feel confident that I will have a life filled with love and peace after his passing.

On other days, grief takes over. I listen to music that is sad and let the tears stream down my checks as I run. *My Immortal* by Evanescence is my go-to song for tears. I am swallowed up on these runs by a sea of raging emotions. I run harder, faster and longer until I can no longer cry and the emotions are gone. I hide behind dark sunglasses so my neighbors will not see my tears.

I always return home sweaty and exhausted, but filled with the energy needed to care for my family. We have fallen into a routine this month. Vince wakes for the second time between noon and 2 p.m. He is still able to shower by himself, one of the few acts of independence he has left. Showers take a while and leave him depleted of energy. He dresses and then lies on the bed for several hours trying to build up the strength to climb the stairs down to the living room. Most afternoons he will fall back asleep and wake when Kate brings him an ice tea. This precious time with Kate always makes him happy. These moments are evidence that moving in was the right decision.

One afternoon early in the month, I stop by Vince's room to spend some time with him. He is beginning to experience loneliness because he is spending his days in bed. Sometimes he just wants someone to sit with him. I bring my laptop to his room and sit in the bed while sending out emails and working on projects. Today he looks so forlorn and exhausted.

I am clicking away on my computer when I hear him softly whisper, "I want to go home to see my family one last time."

His words surprise me, and initially I am annoyed. I moved in so he could spend quality time with James and Kate, and now he wants to leave again to go be with his family. But then I separate his actions from him. I know he must need some attention and emotional support. The kids and I are busy with school and work. I also realize that I only provide him with physical care. I am not far enough along on my path towards forgiveness to provide the emotional support he wants.

Guilt washes over me. If I were better at caring for him, maybe he would stay and spend more time with the children. But I quickly rationalize in my head that I have already given so much and I'm just not ready to let him in emotionally. On some level, I am hoping Vince takes responsibility for the actions that have distanced him from his children. But he continues to be focused on his own pain and grief.

Once again, I separate his actions from who he is. He needs something I can't provide, and the silver lining is that I will have a break from the role of caregiver.

"Of course. I'll help you with whatever you need," I tell him.

***

A couple of days later I drive him to the airport for his flight to Philadelphia. He instructs me to drop him at the curb. He slowly climbs out of the car as I retrieve his bag from the trunk. I want him saving his energy for the potentially long walk through the airport. I offer to make the trip with him and fly back home the next day. However, he is determined to make this last trip alone, one last act of independence. I try to arrange a wheelchair and a transporter to take him to the gate, but he insists on walking. Chicago is such a large airport, and I am concerned that he will wear himself out. Vince is a proud man and refuses to use a wheelchair. For the first time ever he has had to check his bag. He is too weak to wheel it through the airport.

I reach up and give him a hug goodbye. "Safe travels," I say. "I'll text you when I land."

He is tired, and I am fearful he will pass away while home with his family. He is weak, and I'm not sure how much more fight he has left in him.

He makes it to Philadelphia safely and begins what we think will be a two-week visit. I'm sure he feels comforted being in his childhood home with his mother. Don't we all want our mothers when we are sick? She cooks all his favorite foods—chicken soup, homemade pizza, eggplant parmesan, osso buco and chicken cutlets. His afternoons are spent swimming in the pool. In the evenings, his mother hosts dinners or they eat at some of Vince's favorite restaurants. Vince's mother is retired, so she is able to devote all her time to Vince, and he soaks up all the love. He is having a terrific time, and I can hear the happiness in his voice when I speak with him.

Back in Chicago, the kids and I are enjoying a break from Vince's cancer. Things almost feel normal, and we eagerly return to our regular routines. I am able to spend time at the office and participate in meetings. James and Kate relish getting together with their friends without feeling guilty they are taking time away from Vince. I plug back in with my friends and neighbors, too, and accept every invitation that comes my way.

July 8, 2012

Today I spent the day with myself. Something I have not done in a long time. The house is so quiet. James is working, and Kate is with her friends for the day. The solitude is a blessing. I sit on the deck and enjoy a delicious bottle of wine. My neighbor's bird feeders are a flurry of activity. I am aware that this time next year Vince will be gone and my life will be completely different.

I haven't heard from Vince very much since he has been with his family. Selfishly, I am relishing the break from my role as caretaker. I've been fighting to control what is happening to our family and I am exhausted. This day of solitude is a blessing.

***

Vince is at the end of his two-week trip and he calls to say he is extending his stay for another week. He feels incredible and is having such a good time that he wants to remain longer. Both the kids and I encourage him to remain at his mother's home. His phone call is cheerful and he has renewed energy. Unfortunately, he only took enough medication for two weeks, so I overnight his drugs to him for the next week.

I am so excited to have another week to myself. But in the recesses of my mind I know why Vince feels so good and I am worried. I have read about this very moment in the hospice information. Terminally ill patients often experience a burst of energy labeled "rallying" before the end. The timing and duration can vary from patient to patient. Rallying moments can last for days or sometimes a week or more. I have such mixed emotions. I am so pleased he is feeling invigorated, but I suspect the end will follow closely.

***

At the close of his third week with his family, I receive a very animated phone call from Vince. He is feeling amazing. He can't believe how good he feels and how much energy he has. He is convinced the chemotherapy treatments were the reason he felt so terrible. It has been almost 10 weeks since his last chemo cocktail. His only complaint is that food is beginning to stick in his esophagus again. He is upset because the doctor told him the stint would last until he passed. He is feeling so great that he announces he is considering having radiation on his esophagus so he can eat better.

I am in shock. I remember how miserable he was the last time he had radiation. It was at the top of his spine. The radiation penetrated part of his esophagus creating internal blistering that was unbearable.

"Just make sure you are really up for all the side effects and complications," I say. "Remember last time? You told me that even if they promised you that you would live 10 more years if you had radiation, you would say no. Remember, how painful it was? They weren't even concentrating the radiation on your esophagus."

We had always discussed Vince's wishes. From the beginning, he has been committed to having quality time with his family and friends, not pursuing quantity of time. We always discussed weighing the benefits of treatment against the pain and complications or the time spent away from the family if he doesn't feel well.

I am afraid of the type of care he will require and I know how sick he will be. The radiation will leave his esophagus raw. I remember back to the time he wanted to end his life because of the pressure he felt from the stint implantation. Vince's decision will affect the entire family, especially me. I have to be realistic, but I feel selfish for bursting his fantasy.

I suggest to him that he should stay another week with his family since he is feeling so full of life. I gently encourage him to consider whether he really wants to radiate his esophagus.

I speak with his mother briefly. She is thrilled Vince is flourishing. "I think the good Lord has answered our prayers," she says.

"Yes, I am so happy he is feeling so well," I say. "Hospice told me he would experience a burst of energy like this."

There is silence on the other end. I immediately regret my brutal honesty. It was not my place to say anything. I am not his wife.

"I'm overnighting more medication," I say, trying to change the subject. "And I am so happy that you are all having such a good time together."

I hang up the phone and pray he makes it home before his burst of energy runs out.

CHAPTER TEN

AUGUST — AUTOPILOT

The first week of August Vince flies back to Chicago from Philadelphia. Vince has been feeling so energized, I decide to send James to the airport. I am anticipating an important delivery and don't want to miss it. I have the kitchen door open waiting for the boys to arrive home. Murphy, our dog, sits patiently looking out towards the driveway.

Murphy and Vince have become best buddies. Murphy was a gift to James and Kate the Christmas before we divorced. Murphy has made the transition to living in Vince's home effortlessly. Being a West Highland Terrier who loves to chase chipmunks and squirrels, I'm sure he misses his big yard.

When we first moved in and Vince was not yet feeling the effects of his cancer, they would go on long walks each day. Vince enjoyed feeding and walking Murphy. This gave him something to do each afternoon and evening as he waited for everyone to arrive home from school and work.

His attachment became very evident over the summer. Murphy had eaten some rib bones that James had left on the coffee table in the basement, the remnants of a midnight snack. Rib bones are very dangerous for dogs because they can splinter in their digestive track. Murphy came to my room one evening and collapsed on my floor. He would suddenly stand and stretch his neck as if he were in pain then collapse on the floor again. We realized quickly that Murphy had eaten the leftover rib bones. We rushed him to the 24-hour emergency vet. We were not the most serious case at the clinic, so we waited to see a doctor almost three hours just to be told it was too late to retrieve the bones. They were already traveling through his digestive track. We would have to wait it out.

We were all very concerned and worried for Murphy, but Vince took it to an extreme. He sobbed when I told him that we would just have to hope for the best that the rib bones didn't splinter and perforate Murphy's intestine. He turned all his anger and rage on James.

"This will be all your fault if he dies. This will be on your conscience," Vince screamed.

I'm sure James already felt bad enough, and Vince's tirade further widened the gap between them emotionally.

Each day James drove Murphy to the vet to be X-rayed, to see where the bones were in his digestive track. Finally, on day three, he eliminated the last of the bone fragments. Vince and I were walking Murphy when I announced the good news. Vince grabbed me and hugged me as he began to cry.

"I really thought he was going to die. I am so happy. I love this little dog and I don't know what I would do without him."

I'm brought back to the present when James pulls into the driveway. Murphy bounds out to the car. He excitedly dances outside the passenger door wagging his tail.

"Hey, Murph," Vince says, scratching his ears. "How you doing Buddy? I missed you."

I walk out to the car. "Hey, Vince," I say.

He looks up at me weakly, and I can tell something is wrong. James climbs out of the car and announces he must get ready for work. He quickly heads into the house avoiding the realities of Vince's situation. Vince continues to sit in the car.

"It's going to take me a while to get inside," he whispers.

I place my hand on his shoulder. "Take your time. I'm not going anywhere."

He begins to weep. "I barely made it out of the airport. I have no strength. I had to stop several times and steady myself. I could barely get off the airplane. I was really scared they would need to call the paramedics." He slowly swings his legs out of the car and sits on the edge of the passenger seat. Murphy stands up to lick Vince's face.

My heart swells with compassion, and I can feel a lump form in my throat. I know the downward slide is beginning, and the end is moving closer. After a long while, Vince grips the passenger door to pull himself up. He is wearing shorts. His legs are thin and frail. He is very unsteady on his feet. He stands for a couple of minutes trying to gather more strength to make the short walk to the kitchen door and step into the house.

"I'm exhausted. I just want to go to bed."

Murphy and I shadow him. He pauses as he reaches the steps into the house. He grips the doorway with both hands and leans against it.

"It's going to take me a few minutes to get inside."

I place my hand on his back. "Take your time."

A couple of minutes later he takes a deep breath and summons forth all the energy he can to climb the two stairs into the kitchen.

"I'm going to need to rest before I can go upstairs." He moves slowly towards the family room to sit in a chair where he leans back and closes his eyes. He looks beaten.

"Have you eaten today?" I ask.

He just shakes his head no. I retrieve a protein drink and straw from the kitchen and hold it for him while he takes sips.

"I just don't know how much longer I can go on," he sighs. Just a day ago in Philadelphia he had boundless energy. We are both aware that this is the beginning of his decline.

Almost an hour later, he slowly climbs the stairs one by one to his bedroom. He crawls into bed and sleeps most of the afternoon. That night he has no appetite, but Kate manages to convince him to eat an ice-cream sundae. She sits with him, and they talk about Vince's visit with his family.

While sugar is the worst thing for any cancer patient to eat, at this point it is just important he eats something.

***

August 10, 2012

> *Last night I could not sleep. I am so worried about Vince. The doctor said he would probably make it to Labor Day, now just two weeks away. My heart aches for James and Kate. Will they be able to watch their father die at home? I had no idea what a sacrifice this was going to be, not only for me but also for the kids. Have I done the right thing, making us live together as a family?*

I head to Vince's room early to help him with his medications. He is growing weaker and has trouble opening the various bottles of pills. His meds include 14 pills each morning and night. Midday he takes another group of pills. In between, he takes morphine as needed for pain management.

He sits on the edge of his bed, and I hand him the pills two at a time. It takes a while for him to swallow all his medications.

"I heard you coughing this morning. Is everything okay?" I ask.

"I couldn't stop coughing. I coughed up some stuff into the sink. I left it there for you to look at."

I step into the bathroom. There are little brown granules in some mucous. Our hospice nurse is scheduled for a visit today so I decide to show it to her, but deep down inside I know the news will not be good.

"I'm going to leave this in the sink so the nurse can see it."

"What is it?" he asks.

"I'm sure it's nothing to worry about," I lie. "Let's let the nurse take a look. I'm sure she will know what it is."

Later that afternoon our nurse arrives with another nurse. While the second nurse takes Vince's vitals I bring our regular nurse upstairs to look in the sink. She looks in, takes a breath and frowns.

"This isn't good."

"What is it?"

"It's called coffee grounds. It means he is bleeding in his stomach."

"I was afraid of that." In our hospice literature, I had read about coffee grounds, and I knew this was not a good thing.

I look her in the eye. "How long? Be honest with me. I need to be prepared."

"If he continues spitting up coffee grounds, probably a couple of weeks." The news jars me, and my eyes pool with tears.

We've known from the beginning that Vince will eventually die, but I am still surprised that the end is so close. Grief overwhelms me.

"I'm so sorry." The nurse touches my arm.

"It's okay. I just really need you to be honest with me about what might happen next."

"So the coffee grounds indicate bleeding somewhere, probably his stomach. His tumors may rupture at any moment, and he will bleed out. I will send over a triage kit today just in case."

I feel like someone has just punched me in the stomach, and I want to crumble. Triage kit? The words sound scary.

"Are you okay," the nurse asks again.

I nod yes. "It's just so sad."

I am sad for Vince whose life will be cut short. I am sad for James and Kate who will lose their father at too young an age. I am sad for Vince's mother who will have to bury her son.

I take a deep breath and head downstairs. It is time for me to be the rock for my family. Time to share the news with Vince.

We haven't even rounded the corner into the dining room, when Vince eagerly asks, "So what is it?"

"It's coffee grounds."

He looks at the nurse and asks, "What does that mean? How much longer do I have?"

"You are bleeding internally. The coffee grounds indicate blood, which is probably from your stomach. Generally when we see coffee grounds, it's not very long. Maybe a couple of weeks."

Vince bends over and grips the dining room table. His arms look like thin noodles of spaghetti. Fear washes over his suntanned face. This news is an absolute blow. The certainty of death is now just weeks away. Behind his glasses I can see his eyes tear up and his face begin to twist.

His voice cracks, and he shakes his head. "I thought I had more time."

The room is silent. There is nothing anyone can say at this moment to make him feel better.

"I just wish I had more time," he says.

I move to his side and drape my arm around his shoulders. As he sobs, tears stream down my face, too.

"Don't worry. I will be with you. We will get through this together."

At this point in our relationship my empathy and compassion outweigh any animosity I might still harbor. I no longer view Vince as my ex-husband but instead as a human being who is dying and deserves comfort, solace and a loving touch. While the anger and resentment are not completely gone, there is no longer room for these feelings in my daily thoughts.

The hospice staff comforts Vince and assures us that they are available for anything we need.

Vince is absolutely devastated. "I'm really tired," he says.

He slowly rises and steadies himself against the dining room table to begin the long ascent up the stairs. One of the hospice nurses offers to shadow him to his room and help him settle into bed.

Climbing the stairs requires a herculean effort on Vince's part. He must climb one stair at a time and rest in between. When he reaches the landing, it is necessary for him to rest for several minutes. When he finally arrives at the top, he feels like he has just climbed Mount Everest. It is distressing to watch him struggle so much.

Once Vince is in his room, I ask the nurse what to expect moving forward.

"He will begin to sleep much more and he may become confused as the toxins build up in his system. There may be more coffee grounds. His appetite will decline, and you should be prepared that he may bleed out. He may become more agitated. I will come by tomorrow with a triage kit for bleeding out."

"What is a triage kit?" I ask.

"We will explain it tomorrow when it's dropped off. It is stuff you will need when he bleeds out."

"He is having surgery tomorrow to check his stint," I tell her. "He is having a lot of trouble swallowing, so they are scoping him to see what is happening. Tomorrow will be a long day for him. Why don't you come by the following afternoon? I will call you if I need anything."

It was up to me to make sure Vince was cared for in the best possible way, and that Kate and James were emotionally prepared for their father's death. Over the last eight months, I have always deferred decision-making regarding Vince's health to him. After all, I wanted him to feel empowered as long as possible. He needed to continue to feel like he was capable. But he was exhausted now. Making day-to-day decisions regarding his care would now become my responsibility. It would be up to me to work with hospice to make sure all of Vince's needs were met. Most importantly, I would be responsible for healthcare decisions if something should go wrong during surgery. Even though I knew eventually I would have to make decisions regarding his care, the reality of the burden suddenly feels very heavy.

***

Later in the afternoon, he begins sharing the news with everyone. I sit in his room as he makes phone calls. He tells people the end is near and that if they would like to visit him, they should come now.

It is heart wrenching watching Vince make these calls. He is exhausted but manages to rally the strength to reach out to everyone who has expressed an interest in visiting him. He has asked people to coordinate their travel with me. Friends and family begin making flight arrangements, and I field phone calls as they confirm schedules.

The list of visitors grows too long for me to keep in my mind, so the kitchen blackboard becomes command central. There are five days listed and under each day is a list of 10 to 12 visitors. People are flying in from all over the U.S., and Vince's mother will be flying in, as well.

"We need to have food when people arrive," Vince says.

"Of course. I will take care of everything."

Fortunately, I am enjoying rediscovering my passion for cooking and I begin preparing menus for each day. I am in my element organizing and entertaining.

After all the calls are made, Vince lies back in bed. He is emotionally drained and weak. Kate drops by his room and manages to convince him to have an ice-cream sundae with her. I leave them alone to chat. I am so happy that she is taking advantage of spending time with her father. No matter how terrible he feels, he lights up when she walks into his room.

***

The following morning, we prepare for Vince's doctor to scope him and take a look at the stint. A couple of weeks ago while in Philadelphia, Vince had begun to feel like food was sticking in his esophagus again. The surgeon had assured us that it would remain unobstructed and that Vince would be able to eat until the very end. We are eager to find out what the scope will reveal. I am worried about this surgery. Vince is weak, and I wonder if he will have the strength to make it through. What if the tumor ruptures while they are scoping him? I am incredibly nervous but put on a strong face for everyone.

We arrive at the hospital and park in the parking structure. Vince refuses to allow me to call for a wheelchair. We must walk very slowly to the surgery floor. Vince is unstable and so weak that we stop often so he can steady himself against the wall. I used to be annoyed when he would refuse to make things easier for not only himself but also for me. But I now understand he is just trying to hold on to himself. These last acts of independence are his way of holding tightly to life. How can I take those things away from him? I don't have that right. Again, grace and patience override any feelings of frustration.

Fortunately, the staff immediately takes us back to prepare him for the surgery. He sits on the edge of the bed for a while without moving.

He looks up at me with a forlorn expression. "I'm going to need your help."

"Of course." I smile warmly and give him a hug.

I slowly help him undress and carefully bag his clothes. His body has begun to atrophy, and his arms are painfully thin. He has used all his energy to walk to the surgery and he can barely stand at this point. I manage to put a hospital gown on him and once again remove his Blessed Mother medallion.

Exhausted, he lies back in the bed and closes his eyes. I know he is worried he may not come out of the surgery. He is tired of fighting, feeling sick and taking medication.

We sit in silence. The air is heavy with all the words we have yet to speak to one another. There is so much left unsaid between us. My phone buzzes constantly with text messages from James, Kate and family and friends all wondering how surgery is going.

The nurse arrives to wheel Vince to the operating room. I stand quickly and move to his bed. He is petrified. I squeeze his hand and place my other hand over his heart and stare directly into his eyes. In the past I had avoided eye contact with Vince, but now I let my guard down. He needs reassurance so he can focus on surviving the surgery.

"I will see you in an hour." I raise my eyebrows to let him know I mean business. "You are going to be fine, and we will all have ice cream tonight. Okay?"

He nods, and I reach down to kiss his cheek.

"See you when you wake up."

As they wheel him away, I am shaken. I really don't have confidence that he will survive the surgery. He is so weak.

I walk to the family waiting area. Only one other family is there. I sit down and stare at his name on the board. I am suddenly overwhelmed with the feeling of a bright orange and yellow light. It is a warm and comforting light that makes me smile. I take a deep breath and peace fills me.

I stare again at his name on the board. My heart is filled with love for him as my children's father and a human being. I am aware that I have let go. I no longer feel it is my place to judge him. He was not equipped with the skills he needed in this life to be a good husband and father, but that doesn't mean he has to leave this life feeling unloved. I am resolved to make every minute of these next few weeks the best for him and for my children.

***

Ninety minutes later, I am summoned back to see Vince. The surgery was a success. Apparently, the stint had shifted position and had slid into his stomach. The stint had become dislodged when he ate sticky bread items that pulled the stint down into his stomach. The surgeon removed the old stint and repositioned a new stint back in his esophagus. The upside is that he will now be able to eat again without food getting stuck in his esophagus. The downside is that the painful pressure from the stint has returned to his chest.

***

Later that night, Vince surmises that the stint was displaced during his birthday weekend with all the cake, bread and pastries he ate. I ask him how he knows this. He says that the pain in his chest from the stint went away halfway through that weekend. It's an absolute miracle that he has been able to eat during this time.

He is awake most of the night with pain. He continues to cough, a side effect from the anesthesia and stint. I run down to his room several times to check on him. The surgery has left him weak, and the constant pain steals what little energy he has left. We are scheduled to take James to college tomorrow, and I am very concerned that this trip will be too much for Vince.

James has been busy this month preparing to depart for the University of Cincinnati in Ohio. There were not enough dorms this year for incoming freshmen, so James will be living in an apartment near campus with three other roommates he does not know. Moving him into an apartment adds another level of complexity to the college process. I manage to convince James to go shopping one afternoon to purchase bedding and some supplies for his new place; however, I know there is much more he needs. James is handling all the packing himself, and I try very hard to let him figure it out. I wonder if Vince were feeling better, would he be helping James prepare for college. Their relationship is still so tenuous that I'm not sure.

James comes up in the morning to visit Vince, and I leave them to talk. It's a short visit, and James finds me afterwards to share his concern that Vince is too weak to make the trip. It's a long drive and James' apartment is located on the fifth floor. We have been given a move in time of 8 a.m. This means we must make the six-hour drive the day before and stay in a hotel. It will be an uncomfortable trip for Vince. The plan was to let Vince sleep at the hotel the following morning and then bring him over in the afternoon to see James' apartment and say goodbye. He simply will not have the strength to help James move in.

"Mom," James says, "Dad is still determined to come. He is so weak. I am worried that he will collapse in the hall, and we will have to call the paramedics. I told him that if he can't make the trip that it would be okay. You have to convince him not to come."

James has no idea that I have spent the last few days trying to persuade Vince that the drive and the amount of walking we will need to do will be too much for him to handle. He is determined to see James settled in at college and his apartment. It's a milestone he will never have the opportunity to experience with Kate.

***

The next morning I wake early and go for a run to clear my head. I listen to an energizing playlist that fills me with adrenaline. I try to harness my excitement around James departing for school. This should be a fun time for him, and I am trying to make it feel as normal as possible. I hear the shower go on in Vince's bathroom around ten. James comes up from the basement.

"Is he still coming?" James asks.

"Yes. Don't worry. I will make sure you get settled. You let me handle your Dad. You just make sure you have packed everything."

James begins the process of packing both our cars for the trip. About 30 minutes later, I hear Vince's bedroom door open, and he calls down for me.

"Coming," I call. I head up the stairs to his room. He is sitting on the edge of his bed in a T-shirt and boxers.

"I can't make the trip." He looks at the floor and shakes his head.

I am honestly relieved to hear this news. However, I see the pain in his face and hear the sadness in his voice. He is devastated. I sit beside him on the bed and place my hand on his knee.

"It's okay. James will understand."

"Can you ask him to come up before you leave?"

"Of course. He is just finishing packing the cars."

I'm suddenly aware that I need to make arrangements for someone to stay with Vince. There is no way I can leave Kate home alone to care for him. She has recently been diagnosed with mononucleosis. She must rest up so she can start school next week. I also remember how difficult it was for James when he took care of Vince in June.

I am trying to put Vince's needs first, but I am angry that he has waited until the last minute to decide not to go. I knew yesterday he would not have the strength to make the trip. I broach the subject of sending a nurse to stay at the house while I am away. I remind him that Kate is sick and needs rest. He becomes angry and assures me that he will be fine.

At this point, I am unglued. There is no way I can leave Kate alone with Vince. I have to find someone who Vince will allow to come to the house and be here for him instead of Kate. I call Vince's best friend, who lives in Chicago, and ask for his help. He agrees to call Vince later in the afternoon and pretend he wants to come out to visit. Once he is at our house, he will simply just stay over until I return home the next evening.

I send James upstairs to say goodbye to Vince. Vince had planned to come along, so he and James had planned to say goodbye in Cincinnati. There is a very real possibility that James may not see Vince again. No one wants to acknowledge this overwhelming thought.

James comes downstairs a couple of minutes later. "You need to go upstairs," he says. "Dad is a mess. He's hysterical."

I climb the stairs two at a time and find Vince standing in the middle of his bedroom sobbing uncontrollably. He is so overwrought with emotion that he cannot speak.

"It's okay," I say and give him a hug.

"Please tell him I love him and I am so proud of him."

I can barely understand Vince as he continues to sob. I don't understand why he can't say these things to James himself.

"Thank you for taking our son to college. You are the best mother." He hugs me.

"I'll check in with you later."

I am so thankful he is not attempting to make the trip, but I am also sorry for him that he will not have the pleasure of seeing his son off to school like other fathers. Vince is despondent, and I understand how grief stricken he is. But I wish he could acknowledge how James may be feeling instead of focusing on his own loss. Vince should share how proud of him he is and how excited he is for him to be going off to college. I can't imagine what must be going through James' mind. He may never see his father again. For most students, departing for college is a happy and exciting time, but for James it is tarnished with impending grief.

***

I embrace my excitement for James to begin his college career and I focus on making the next 24 hours as normal and fun as possible for James. He is taking his car to school, so we drive separately.

I check in with Kate via phone several times during the long road trip. Of course, there is one crisis after another with Vince. My anger begins to build. Why hasn't Vince's friend shown up yet? Vince assured me he did not need anyone to take care of him, but here he is having Kate run up and down the stairs managing one crisis after another. At one point, Vince clogs one of the bathroom toilets and Kate has to shut off the water and unstop the toilet with a plunger. His selfishness in refusing a nurse has put undo stress on Kate and myself. I feel terrible that I have left her behind.

Vince refuses to let his friend come out to visit because he is not feeling well. So my plan for having him spend the night at the house has evaporated. My stress level is off the charts. I am angry that no one is respecting the plan.

I treat James to a steak dinner in Cincinnati but I am consumed with worry for Kate and what her night with Vince will hold.

***

We wake up early and head to James' apartment building. We quickly move in all the items we have already purchased; however, there is still much more to buy. We go to Target. I am trying to enjoy my time with James but I am riddled with worry. He is excited to be at school, and I am so thrilled to see him get started.

James makes me a proposition. If I agree to make up his bed, he'll carry all the bags up from the car. What a deal.

He finishes bringing in the last of the bags as I toss the pillows on his bed. "Thanks Mom," he gives me hug. "So I guess you can go."

"Are you sure you don't want me to help you with anything else?" I ask. I'm not ready to leave him just yet.

"No. I can finish moving the rest of my stuff in. Thanks though."

I understand his need for independence, and I know I should probably start the long drive home. I give him another hug and wish him much success. I am filled with gratitude that he is safely ensconced at school where he can begin to forge his own destiny.

It is a sunny day, and the roads are free of traffic. On the drive home James texts me pictures of his apartment as he finishes setting things up.

Vince's best friend, the one who didn't come yesterday, has come today. While I am annoyed he did not follow our original plan, I am grateful for his help. I check in periodically on the way home, and Vince seems to be in better spirits. When I arrive, I share with him the photos James has sent me. He is still sad he could not be a part of this milestone but is happy knowing James is settled.

***

It is the first day of Kate's senior year, another milestone. I am working very hard to make sure Kate has no additional pressure placed on her so she can stay focused on school. She needs to keep her GPA up and complete her college applications.

Aside from helping James move, I have been tethered to the house since Vince returned from Philadelphia. I have juggled working from home, taking care of Vince, managing Kate's mononucleosis and preparing James to leave for college.

Today my business partner and I are giving a major presentation to more than 30 participants for a very important client. It involves the launch of a new business vertical for our company, and I have been preparing for this day for months. Vince's best friend has agreed to spend the day with Vince, so I can work without interruption. It feels great to be out of the house and engaged in work. Our presentation goes well, and on the way home I check in with Vince. He is having a good day, and his friend is planning to stay for dinner. I ask Vince if he minds if I stop and have a late lunch with my business partner.

"Absolutely. Take your time. I'm going to dinner with my friend."

I am satisfied that Vince is in good hands and I can have a much-needed break. We head to my business partner's house where we have a quick bite and a beer to celebrate. She can see how much stress I am under and she suggests we take a swim. I welcome the break and slide into the water.

We've both left our phones inside the house. I haven't checked in with Vince in a couple of hours, and he begins calling my phone looking for me. He leaves multiple messages over the course of an hour. He begins to worry and enlists Kate's help to track me down. She assures Vince I am with my business partner at her house and that I'm just fine. She explains that I often hang out at her house after an important meeting and that I will be home soon.

He begins to panic that I have been in a car accident. He calls my business partner's cell phone and leaves frantic messages looking for me. Kate calls my business partner's daughter to ask if she knows where we are.

Vince demands Kate drive to my business partner's house and make sure I am there. We are in the pool when she arrives. She explains that Vince is freaked out and that I need to come home right away. I hurry inside to change as my partner picks up a call from Vince on her phone.

He screams at her. "Do you know I am dying? Where is Karen? She hasn't checked in for hours. I don't need this kind of stress. I am a dying man."

Thankfully my partner remains calm. "Kate is here, and Karen is fine. They're both on their way home."

Of course, he mentions nothing to my business partner about his concern for me. This really is about the fact that I took some time off from giving him my undivided attention. His ego is in full swing, but I feel completely detached from any emotion about it.

When I arrive home, his best friend is still with him. Vince is totally calm and composed.

"Everything okay?" I ask, smiling and raising an eyebrow.

"Yes." He smiles and looks at the TV as if nothing has happened. Normally, this response would enrage me and make me think of the past, but I am separated from his behavior.

"Okay," I say. "But your voicemails on my phone were pretty frantic."

He raises his voice. "Do you have any idea how worried I was about you? You didn't check in for hours, and I was so worried you were in an accident. What would I do if something happened to you? I need you. I need to know where you are in case I need your help."

It was clear at that moment that Vince was incredibly dependent on me.

The irony of the situation is that I spent most of our married life not knowing where he was on any given night. I never knew which city he was traveling to or where he was each day. When he was in town, I never knew if he would be home for dinner. When I asked about it, he would tell me that I wasn't his mother and he didn't have to check in with me. I looked at the situation a little differently. I was his partner and I felt it should be a common courtesy for him to let me know if he is coming home for dinner or not. Now, with the tables turned I can't help myself.

"So now you know how it felt for me all those years when I never knew where you were."

"I'm dying, and that's what you want to bring up?" He glares at me.

Once again, he is incapable of considering anyone else's emotions.

"I'm just saying." I shrug and turn to leave the room. Even though I have forgiven and have learned to detach from his behavior, I couldn't resist pointing out the irony of the situation. I just wanted him to recognize the similarities.

***

I am pleased that Vince's mother is coming. I will have help preparing meals and caring for Vince. The next week will be very busy with visitors arriving each day to say goodbye to him.

August 26th through August 30th is a whirlwind of friends and business associates. Each day we host up to 10 people throughout the day for lunch, dinner and cocktails. Visiting hours start in the early afternoon. This allows Vince to sleep all morning and conserve his energy. He is touched by the outpouring of sympathy and manages to rally. Reliving his career through the eyes of his peers has filled him with energy and life. I appreciate hearing all the stories, as well, and I am reminded of what a successful career he has had.

Everyone who visits Vince cannot believe how well he looks. He does not look like a typical cancer patient, even though he is at the end of his battle. He has a suntan from his month in Philadelphia, and all his hair has grown back.

I enjoy seeing Vince in such good spirits, and I relish the opportunity to reconnect with many of his friends whom I have not seen since our divorce. Laughter and activity fill the house, and for a moment we all forget why we have come together.

***

Vince comes down to the kitchen to have coffee in the afternoon, and we replay the activity of the last four days. He is thrilled so many people have stopped by to say goodbye.

"Thank you so much for hosting everyone this week," he says. "Everyone really enjoyed eating your cooking again. It felt like old times. Didn't it?"

I smile wide and nod my head in agreement. A sense of fulfillment spreads over me.

"Well, I should go shower," he says. "The guys will be here soon." As he leaves the kitchen, Vince turns back and says, "I love you."

Without thinking, I look up from the table.

"Love you, too."

A moment of shock settles in after I realize what I have just said. It was such an honest moment, and I do love him. Not as my husband, but as the father of our children. I love him for just being a human being. With forgiveness comes the ability to stop judging. I just accept him for who he is. I am finally at peace with our past. It is time to move forward so we can both move on. I am content and full of grace.

CHAPTER ELEVEN

SEPTEMBER — TIME RUNS OUT

September 1, 2012

> *I wake this morning drained from the last four days of hosting visitors and cooking nonstop. I am excited because Vince's brother is arriving and I know he will be such a great help. He'll go grocery shopping and spend time with Vince. He is a wonderful cook, and I am sure he will want to prepare dinners while he is here. I am so relieved to have some help. I just need to get through the next four hours. Help is on the way!*

***

Our house is again filled with very close friends and family. It's another day of delicious food, cocktails, stories and laughter. Vince has made the gut-wrenching decision that this is the last weekend he will have visitors. He is tired and hasn't been able to sleep as much with all of the daily activity.

He has asked me to begin managing his phone for him. He is having trouble seeing and does not have the energy to talk. I begin answering his phone and replying to texts. I change his voicemail to say he is no longer accepting calls but that people are welcome to call me for updates. I add chief communications officer to my list of many duties these days. Vince has become more and more reliant on me, and I take my responsibility to care for him very seriously. Keeping him comfortable and happy is my primary duty.

He has made it to Labor Day Weekend. Vince knows this is the last time that he will see his buddies from South Carolina. He finds it increasingly difficult to climb the stairs. He now goes downstairs once late in the afternoon and then climbs the stairs just once later in the evening. So this morning he invites his friends to visit him in his room. Vince spends some time with each of them, saying goodbye. He gifts each friend with a very special memento from his personal belongings. He talks to them about "time running out" and he encourages them to enjoy life now. He thanks his friends for being a part of his life and asks them to please stay in contact with James and Kate.

"I won't be here to help guide them. They will need your support."

This same day, James arrives home from college. He has come home to say goodbye. The house is filled with 10 people milling about and watching football. I am busy preparing food, drinks and running up and down the stairs to administer medication and check on Vince periodically. The house is filled to capacity. I am sleeping on an air mattress outside of Vince's room. I have given my room up so Vince's mom and brother have beds. Vince wakes up every couple of hours at night, and my sleep is broken. I function on autopilot.

***

The following morning, Vince asks to speak with James before he returns to school. My heart is heavy for James. My greatest hope was that over the past few months Vince and James would find some peace before Vince passed, but it is not to be. Vince speaks to James about his desire for him to finish college and that he is sad he'll miss graduation. He speaks of wanting James to remember him as a great man. He explains to James that he worked very hard all is life to build his career, and he hopes that James will do the same. He encourages James to reach out to his friends and business associates and to listen to the stories that they will share about him.

"Listen to them. They will tell you what a great man I was."

It was a tough conversation filled with lots of tears for both of them. Time has run out. They hug, and James joins the family for a quick breakfast before he leaves for school. Vince is too weak to come downstairs.

Vince's brother and mother have just returned from mass so we all sit down to a breakfast of blueberry pancakes, bacon, sausage and mixed berries. I try to keep the mood light, talking about school and James' drive back. Vince's mom and brother have stopped at the grocery store to purchase several bags of groceries for James. The mood is somber as he departs. He will head to Cincinnati knowing he may never see his father again.

***

On Monday afternoon, the house is quiet again. Just Vince's mother, brother and best friend from Chicago remain. Everyone is downstairs reading or watching television. I climb the stairs every hour to check on Vince.

Mid afternoon, I am able to persuade Vince to drink some apple juice. I sit on the edge of his bed and hold the straw for him.

"I can't do this anymore," he says. He looks at me with such sadness. "I am so weak and tired. I just want to be done. I'm so afraid."

Vince is incredibly anxious about the manner in which he will die. There is a strong possibility that his tumors will rupture, and he will bleed out.

The triage kit includes a large bin with goggles, gloves, gown, trash bags, towels and plastic tarps that hospice has provided. We are prepared for the worse-case scenario. I have been warned that it will be a traumatic event. Vince will feel as if he is suffocating and he will probably try to sit up or stand. If that happens, I am supposed to keep him in bed, turn him on his side and comfort him as he bleeds out.

Words cannot capture just how terrified I am. I can only imagine how panic-stricken Vince must be. Vince has asked me to shield his mother from the knowledge of how he will die. At this point, I am unable to leave the house unless Vince's best friend is present, just in case he begins bleeding. This adds a whole new layer of strain to our daily routine.

"I know how tired you are." I hold his hand and rub his arm as we talk.

"I'm taking things into my own hands," he says. "I've got enough pain medication squirreled away to just go to sleep."

I always knew this might be a possibility, especially after his threats in May to take his life while I was in California. Once again confronted with the same conversation, I don't know what to say to comfort him.

"Are you asking for my help? You know I can't help you? Right?" I explain.

"I know. I'm not asking for your help. I'm just telling you what I need to do."

While I refuse to help Vince, I do support his choice. I probably would choose to do the same thing if I were in his place. The thought of bleeding out is too much for him to endure.

Unfortunately, Vince's mother finds out about his plan through a relative. She is furious. She asks me how I can support him in taking his own life. I explain that he is dying and exhausted. He just wants the journey to be over.

Vince and his family are staunch conservative Catholics, and this will go against their beliefs. She immediately shares the news with Vince's brother, and they head upstairs to confront Vince. This is family business, so I do not join them. I feel it is not my place or right to insert my opinion, but I cannot help but listen from down the hall. The conversation is ugly, and I am suddenly overwhelmed with a need to protect Vince and his wishes. I slowly creep down the hallway and stand at attention in the doorway ready to jump to his rescue. I see Vince's expression as he tries to advocate for his own rights. She reminds him that they are Catholic, and if he takes his life, he will not go to heaven.

"I don't think you have to worry about that," Vince says sarcastically.

"Then, Vince, all I can do is pray for your soul." She leans down and kisses his head and leaves the room.

I am sure she is a bundle of emotions, and I am distressed that Vince has had harsh words with his mother. Everyone is on edge. She has won, though. Vince never mentions taking his life again. Instead, he begins the process of starving himself to death. He withdraws from everyone, including me. But I know him better than anyone, and I know exactly what he is planning.

***

I am beyond exhausted. I am emotionally drained, and the stress of being present for everyone, managing the end and juggling work is taking a huge toll. We have begun the "critical care" phase, and it is more grueling than I could have ever imagined. I have to find some help in managing the daily routine of the house so I can focus on caring for Vince.

I send an email late at night to a small group of friends asking for assistance with meals. Asking for help is something that is not easy for me to do, but I am overjoyed when I awake the next morning to find a string of messages. My friends have launched a full-scale "dinner" offensive. They've planned three weeks of meals. I have the most amazing friends, and I am so grateful for their help.

***

It is the Tuesday after Labor Day, and we have made it through the weekend. Vince has asked his brother to take him to the barber for one last haircut.

Sadly, this short outing strips every last bit of Vince's energy from his body. When they return, it takes several minutes to climb out of the car and make it to the garage door entrance of the house.

"I can't make it inside," he says. He leans against the car. "I can't do it."

"Just rest a minute." I suggest.

We are all silent for a long while. The moment is filled with grief and sorrow.

"John," Vince says to his brother. "I'm going to stand in front of the stair and try to lift my foot. When I do, you push me from the back." Vince leans into the doorway and supports himself with his arms.

"When I say, 'go,' push me."

His mother and I stand just inside the kitchen to grab him and steady him.

He stumbles into the house and uses the kitchen counter for support.

"I want to go to bed," he says. "I don't think I can make it up the stairs."

I have learned that it is very important to let Vince make decisions about what he wants to do or what he can do. It is so frustrating for him. He has absolutely no control over his body or life at this point. Each day, something more is taken away from him, and it is important that he feels he has a voice. "What do you want to do?" I ask.

Vince's mom immediately jumps in telling him exactly how we should get him upstairs. She continues making suggestions. I stand in silence waiting for Vince's reaction. I can see him grow agitated.

"Vince, what would you like us to do?" I ask again, trying to diffuse the situation.

Vince's mother keeps talking and trying to make suggestions. She is unaware that Vince is getting confused and annoyed.

"Mom. Just let me relax. I'll tell you when I need you to do something," he snaps.

I feel badly for his mom. She is trying to be helpful, but does not realize that she is stripping him of feeling independent. We eventually are able to help Vince climb the stairs one at a time with many breaks and a lot of patience.

***

Vince's brother leaves for the airport. He is returning home knowing he will not see his brother again. We are all acutely aware that the journey is coming to an end. All visitors have left, except for Vince's mom and best friend.

Kate arrives home from school in the afternoon with two ice teas in hand. This is her afternoon ritual with Vince. She brings him an ice tea and they sit and spend time together talking. This afternoon will be bittersweet as Vince says goodbye to Kate. Like James, he encourages her to use his friends as a resource. Through tears, he expresses his sorrow that on her wedding day, he will not be able to walk her down the aisle. Sadly, every happy milestone for James and Kate will always have a sense of grief attached. Those events will be a reminder that their father was taken from them too early.

***

That Friday, I arrange for Vince to have his last therapeutic massage with hospice. At this point he is too weak to get on the massage table, so he lies in his hospital bed we've had delivered to the home, and the therapist makes the best of it. Afterwards, he sleeps comfortably all afternoon.

Vince's best friend has become a daily fixture at our home. He has been such a great help. He checks in to see if I need anything from the grocery store. His wife has made multiple dishes of egg strata, so we have a healthy breakfast each morning.

Vince's bedroom has become the family gathering spot. We move a small loveseat in and add a card table to act as a desk. Vince's mom reads on the sofa while his friend works from the card table. I am in and out of his room all day checking on him, taking his temperature, administering medicines, trying to keep him hydrated and, most of all, keeping him as comfortable as possible. In the mornings, I field phone calls. In the afternoons, I generally set up a makeshift desk on the extra bed and answer work emails. There are many interruptions and distractions, so work is difficult.

The constant state of limbo is taking a toll on everyone, especially our daughter Kate. She is only 16, and I think she expected that one night her father would go to sleep and not wake up. She is scared what the end will be like. Unfortunately, things don't always work out as we hope. What is that saying? "We make plans, and God laughs."

I pray every night that God continues to keep me strong to follow his plan for Vince's transition. Weeks earlier I had decided I could no longer live in fear. I have accepted that Vince will die; I have no control over how it happens. I am no longer afraid that he will bleed out. I will handle whatever happens as he passes. I am a rock.

Last night before Vince's mom went to bed, she cried. "I pray every night that the Lord takes him," she tells me.

Vince has decided to respect his mother's wishes and not take his own life with medication. What no one knows is that he has been refusing food for many days now. I am overcome with grief for him. He has chosen such a difficult way to die. He prays every night that he won't wake in the morning. He is so very petrified that he will bleed out. He is in constant pain and can barely make it to the bathroom to relieve his bladder. He has stopped moving his bowels, and it is just a matter of time before the toxins begin building up in his brain.

His moments of lucidness are peppered heavily with moments of mumbling. His mind is jumbled and he looks confused most of the time, asking the same questions over and over again. Patience is a necessity to complete this last part of the journey. Being a caregiver at this point requires an absolute willingness to endure.

He has become uncooperative and refuses to take his pills. He is convinced the anti-anxiety medication is stripping him of his energy. Yet he is incredibly anxious and fearful of bleeding out. He is despondent each morning when he wakes up and finds he is still alive. Every interaction is a negotiation with him to take medication, manage his care or support him emotionally.

I have truly underestimated how difficult this would be. It is physically and emotionally grueling to care for someone 24 hours a day. I wonder if Vince realizes what a sacrifice his daughter, his mother and myself are making at this point? I am disappointed that I have not been able to get through to his heart at the end. Does he understand that we have all put our lives on hold to care for him? Sadly, I don't think he can understand all that I have sacrificed to give him the gift of dying at home. It makes me sad that he will leave this earth not understanding how much I gave him. I have failed Vince, my children and God. I was convinced that by moving in he would soften his heart and learn to operate from it. Time has run out for me to make an impact. Grief and guilt fill my heart.

***

Vince has made it one week past Labor Day. Several days ago, I began sleeping in his room at night in his bed while he sleeps in a medical bed. Our nights are long. He wakes every couple of hours and sits up. Each time this happens, I quickly get up and stand in front of him while he sits on the edge of the bed. I want to prevent him from trying to stand. He is usually confused and doesn't really know what he wants. I persuade him to sip some apple juice, and I rub his back until he relaxes and is able to lie back down. This requires repositioning pillows and blankets so he is comfortable. I often stand next to him and rub his head until he falls asleep again.

In the morning he awakes around 4 a.m. "Can you go get my mom?" he asks. "I think I have enough energy for one more shower."

I know that he will lose this burst of energy quickly.

"It's so early, Vince. Why don't I help you?"

Vince manages to walk to the bathroom to pee.

"I don't want you to have to do that."

"It's not a big deal. Listen. We were married for 16 years. I've seen you naked before."

"Yes," he says with a giggle, "but I looked much better back then."

I smile and laugh as I begin preparing the shower. "I promise I won't check you out."

"You won't be seeing much." He laughs again.

He manages the short walk to the shower, climbs in and sits on the tiled shower bench.

"What would you like me to do first?" I ask.

"Wash my hair please."

I step into the shower and pour the shampoo into my hand. I angle the shower head so it covers his body with a warm spray of water. He leans forward to wet his head, and I gently massage his scalp with the shampoo. I wipe his eyes with a washcloth, just like I used to do for James when he was little.

"Now what's next?"

"Can you soap a washcloth and I will wash myself?"

I carefully take his favorite soap and massage the bar with the washcloth. I hand it to him. He can barely hold it in his hand. The weight of the water and soap in the cloth make it too heavy. He rests his hand on his leg and looks up with pleading eyes.

"Here." I softly touch his hand and take the washcloth. "Let me do that for you."

He looks up helplessly. "Thank you."

I am filled with such compassion for him at this moment. How helpless and vulnerable he must feel. By this time I am soaking wet, dressed in running shorts and a tank top. Prior to his shower I had placed two towels in the dryer to warm them up. I run down the hall to retrieve them. I place one towel over his head and another around his shoulders. I gently rub his head to dry the little bit of hair he still has. I then take the towel and dry his legs and feet. He sits limply on the bench looking absolutely bone weary. He takes quite a while to build up the energy to stand and make the short walk to the medical bed. He is so thin, and the skin sags on his body like a poorly altered suit. He slumps onto his bed, and I help him get dressed in a pair of loose shorts and his favorite orange T-shirt. I wash this T-shirt each time he takes it off so it is available as often as possible.

He looks down at the sheets with a puzzled expression.

"I changed them while you were waiting to get dressed."

He just nods and gets back into bed. He sleeps for hours, his strength zapped by his very last shower.

It's been a long two weeks of visitors, and Vince is beginning to require more care each day. I have to write a 15-page proposal for a client that is due next week. It will require a tremendous amount of research and compilation. I am officially struggling to manage my workload. I am so scared that Vince will begin to deteriorate this week, and I am not sure how I will accomplish everything. I am beginning to lose my composure.

I am visibly upset and racing around upstairs doing laundry, answering phone calls and managing our daily routine. Vince calls me into his room. Vince's mother is seated on the small loveseat reading a book.

"Is everything okay?" he asks.

I feel myself begin to unravel. I am trying so hard to take care of everyone and manage everything; there is no room left for work or sleep. He is going to need more care in the next couple of weeks as his health begins to decline. Tears well up in my eyes.

"I'm just really overwhelmed." I fight back tears.

"What can I do for you?"

It's an absurd question. He can barely walk and he is asking what he can do to help.

"Nothing. I have a huge RFQ due next week and I am overwhelmed with the volume of work required to complete it. I just don't know how I will get it done." My voice cracks.

"What is the value of the RFQ? I will write you a check. Then you don't have to worry about getting it done." He offers.

It takes everything I have inside not to crumble. It is just like Vince to make a very bold offer, one that I know is ridiculous and one with which he will never follow through.

My lips quiver as I speak. "It's a $100,000 contract over three years."

"How about I write you a check for $25,000?"

"I just need to focus on getting some work done today."

I turn to Vince's mother and ask if maybe she could help with laundry.

"Of course," she says.

Unfortunately, this does not make me feel any better. The weeks of constant care, added responsibilities and work have taken their toll.

"I'm just so worried about the company losing revenue since I haven't been working very much. There is really nothing you can do," I say. The tears finally begin streaming down my cheeks.

I am so disappointed in myself for falling apart but I have no control over my emotions at this point.

"I'll do anything you want. Just let me know what I can do to help you?" Vince says, trying to reassure me.

"There's nothing you can do right now. Please, just tell me you took care of the house."

"Yes, I did. You and the kids can stay as long as you want with no worries."

"So you took care of redrafting the document so I can stay as long as I want, and I am only responsible for the dues and utilities?"

"Yes. I took care of it." He assures me yet again.

Knowing I have a place to live for the next couple of years without any financial pressure gives me tremendous peace of mind. I don't have to worry about moving the kids again and it gives me time to refocus on my company.

"That helps a lot. I'll be fine. Just having a tough day juggling everything. Thank you."

***

The next few days are filled with Vince reliving his life. He wakes often and looks around the room. At this point, I make sure that there is always someone with him. His mother spends the day reading and waiting for moments that he is awake and lucid. His best friend visits everyday. I am in and out, administering medications and checking on him. Occasionally, he even takes a sip of juice. Kate comes by every afternoon and sits in his room chatting with him if he is awake. We take turns eating dinner downstairs. None of us have the heart to eat in front of him anymore.

I have not slept much in the last four nights and am physically drained. Vince is extremely agitated and so uncomfortable. The toxins are building in his body, and he is now beginning to have trouble communicating.

Tonight he keeps waking and saying, "I want," but he never completes the sentence. All night long he wakes periodically saying the same words over and over again. Suddenly he launches himself out of bed and grabs the fireplace mantle. There is a portable potty chair in front of him with the lid closed. He begins peeing all over the portable potty and the marble fireplace.

"What are you doing?" I ask.

He looks like a small child and does not even acknowledge that he has heard me. He manages to push himself off the fireplace and sit at the very edge of the bed, but he is slipping off. So I stand in front of him and brace his body with mine. I know I am not strong enough to lift him onto the bed.

"Vince, I need you to gather all your strength and try to lift yourself up. I can't lift you."

He gazes at me with the expression of a small boy. I know if he slips to the floor, I will have to call the fire department. My heart swells with compassion. He finally pushes himself back onto the bed just a little more. I reposition his pillows and help him lie back. He closes his eyes.

I begin the task of cleaning up and washing down the fireplace. I am worn out. The house is full of people everyday, but everyone is mired in their own grief unable to do anything other than sit by Vince's bedside. I am wiped out and not sure how much longer I can go without sleep.

I finally drop back into bed, just in time for Vince to wake up again.

He looks over at me. "Do you have the presentation ready?"

"What?" I answer half asleep as I sit up.

"Do you have the presentation ready?" he asks again.

All of a sudden I am aware that Vince is reliving his past. I quickly decide to just go with it. "Yes. I do."

"Great. Does Dave know? Did you call him?"

"Yes. Dave knows."

"Are you sure you are ready?"

"Yes. I have the presentation and I am ready to go."

He then turns and looks at me and leans over slightly. "Who are all these people in the room? I don't know them?"

I smile warmly and answer, "Don't worry. They will introduce themselves before the presentation."

He stares at me for a few seconds and then lays his head back down and closes his eyes. The morning is filled with more of these exchanges. Vince is having flashbacks. I choose to just go with the conversation. There is no reason to upset him. What is most interesting to me is that all these exchanges revolve around work memories. *Is he reliving moments he wishes he could change? Or is he reliving moments he is proud of? Has he replayed any memories from the last 18 years that involve the kids and me?* All of our exchanges are memories from his career. It's as if the rest of us never even existed.

***

Kate is boarding an airplane this afternoon to fly to Philadelphia for the night. Over the summer, Vince's cousin, who is a plastic surgeon, performed an otoplasty, ear surgery on Kate. She is having a minor complication and must return to Philadelphia. She stops in Vince's room to say goodbye, and he wakes up for a moment and recognizes her.

"Call us when you get to Nana's," he instructs her. "Love you."

"Love you, too."

Vince's best friend has come to stay with him while I drive Kate to the airport.

"You're dad is sleeping more and more and I'm not sure when he is going to go," I tell her. "Are you okay if it happens while you are gone?"

"Yes. We said our goodbyes last weekend." She is quiet for a moment as she stares out the window. "Maybe there is a reason why I have to fly to Philadelphia. Maybe I'm not supposed to be home."

Kate is very mature and an old soul. I am proud of the way she is handling this journey with Vince. I drop her at the airport and give her a big hug.

"See you tomorrow night," I say.

"See you tomorrow."

I quickly head home so I can be there when the hospice nurse arrives. Vince wakes while she takes his vitals. He is lucid now and living in the present moment. She asks me to step into the hallway with her.

"So," she says, "it could be anytime now."

My eyes brim with tears.

"He will pass this weekend at some point. His bowel sounds have diminished, and his breath is becoming shallow." She takes my right hand and squeezes it. "How are you doing?"

"I'm exhausted. I haven't slept in four nights. He wakes up every couple of hours and tries to get out of bed. I'm not sure how much longer I can go without sleep?"

"Oh my. You should have told me sooner. I had no idea you were not sleeping. That's not good. You are at the critical care stage. I am sending a night nurse for you tonight. You need to get some sleep."

Tears spill down my face. She hugs me tightly. "Don't worry. You will have help tonight."

We walk back into Vince's room, and she stands next to his bed. She takes his pulse again and he wakes up briefly. She informs him that tonight he will have a nurse. He gives her a confused look.

"Karen is exhausted. She hasn't slept in days and needs to get some sleep tonight. I am sending a nurse to take care of you so she can sleep in her room."

He nods his head in agreement. "I know. I know she is tired."

I walk the hospice nurse out to the driveway. It is a bright sunny Friday, and the neighborhood bustles with activity.

"So, it will be this weekend," she says.

Tears fall yet again. I nod my head in acknowledgment.

"You call me if you need anything. I am actually the on-call nurse Saturday." I am afraid to speak because I know I will lose my composure. I nod my head again, and she gives me a long hug.

"You have done a great job taking care of him. You should be very proud."

"Thank you," I whisper. My feet are cemented to the driveway and I am unable to move. I know the moment I cross the threshold back into the house the countdown will begin. I dread the next 48 hours.

***

I grab my laptop and climb onto the extra bed in Vince's room. His best friend and mother are there, as well. Vince opens his eyes and scans the room. Everyone stops working for a minute and looks at him. I smile at him warmly. He smiles back and closes his eyes.

I receive a text from Kate. I stand up next to Vince's bed and touch his arm. He wakes up for a minute.

"Kate arrived safely and she is at your mother's house," I inform him.

He doesn't open his eyes, but says, "That's good. Everything is going as planned." *Does he mean our plan for Kate? Or is he referring to God's plan for his passing?*

The rest of the afternoon drags on as Vince sleeps. Vince's friend leaves around five for a date night with his wife. Vince's mother and I take turns eating in the kitchen alone.

I have no appetite. I sit in the kitchen forcing myself to eat. My thoughts drift to Vince and that this will be his last Friday with us. He will be gone soon, and our entire life will change yet again.

***

The doorbell rings around eight. It is the night nurse. I had just finished dragging all my bedding back to my room down the hall and had remade the extra bed in Vince's room for her. I take her upstairs to meet Vince. I stand next to his bed and rub his arm to wake him.

"Vince."

He opens his eyes and looks at the nurse standing at the foot of his bed. His eyes open wider. He is confused.

"Vince, this is the nurse who is going to take care of you tonight so I can get some sleep." He looks upset and distraught. The nurse immediately offers to rub his feet and back to help relax him.

Murphy, our dog, has been lying on Vince's bed with me the entire evening. As Vince's mom says goodnight to Vince, she calls Murphy to leave the room. Murphy opens his eyes and just looks at her. He won't move from his spot. Vince's mom tries to lift him off the bed, but he growls at her. He is determined to sleep in Vince's bed that night, something he has never done before. Vince's mother gives up.

I drift off to sleep almost immediately. I am sleeping blissfully when I am awakened by activity in Vince's room around 2:45 a.m. I am shocked to see him uncovered.

The nurse steps out of the bathroom. "He had an accident. I was just changing him and his sheets. I couldn't find another top sheet."

I immediately retrieve a sheet from the closet to cover him. He is very agitated, moving his hands and grumbling. His face twitches uncontrollably.

"Has he been like this all night?" I demand. I am upset. When I went to bed, he was sleeping peacefully.

"No. He has been very quiet all night. He is agitated because I had to move him to change him," the nurse explains.

I sit on the bed next to him and begin rubbing his arm. Murphy is still lying in the same spot just staring at Vince.

"You need to calm down," I say. "Everything is okay. You just had a little accident. Everything is fine now. You need to stop worrying so much. Let me take care of everything. Let me worry now. You need to get some rest. Calm down. Everything will be just fine." I say the same things over and over again. I sit with him for about 30 minutes until he seems to relax.

I bend down and kiss his forehead. "Get some sleep. I'll see you in the morning."

I begin to walk out but turn to call Murphy. He will not budge. I shrug my shoulders and head to my room. By this point, I am completely awake. I make a cup of coffee and grab my laptop to continue working on my proposal. I leave my door ajar so I can hear any activity in Vince's room. About four, I hear Murphy jump off Vince's bed and come down the hall. He curls up in his dog bed. I call him several times to come lie in bed with me, but he refuses.

No more than ten minutes later the nurse appears in my doorway. "He has passed."

"What? I was just with him." I throw on my robe and run down the hall.

A yellow glow from the bathroom lights the room. Vince looks peaceful. I place my hand on his chest unable to believe he is gone. There is no movement. He is absolutely still. I close my eyes and let the tears run down my face.

"Thank you," I say to God and the universe at large.

Vince and I had both been terrified of how traumatic his death would be. This is surely a lesson in surrendering control. I had let go of my fear about how Vince would pass. I trusted the universe to work everything out. The universe worked it out. He passed more peacefully than either of us could have ever hoped.

I glance down the hall at Murphy slumbering away in his bed. Vince's buddy was with him until the very last minute. He must have known that tonight Vince would pass. He showed Vince unconditional love and loyalty until the end.

I head downstairs to tell Vince's mom. As soon as I turn on the light, she knows what has happened. She sits up in bed.

"He's gone?"

"Yes. He just passed. Would you like to come up and say goodbye before the nurse arrives to pronounce the time of death?"

She puts her robe on.

Tears of relief overcome us both. Vince's mom has been with us for the last three weeks watching her son die. It's been a consuming and overwhelming process for her. The grief she feels is deep. She reminds me to remove his medallion, so I gently lift his head. He is still warm to the touch.

"He looks so peaceful," she says.

"He did die peacefully." I bend down and kiss his forehead. "Goodbye. I will miss you." Who would have thought I would ever say those words to Vince, but in this moment, I am filled with love and grace. We are both free to move on to the next phase of our lives, wherever that may be.

I step out into the hall so Vince's mother can have a private moment with him.

A knock at the front door breaks the silence. It is the registered nurse who will pronounce time of death. I show her to Vince's room. The entire hospice staff is so caring and thoughtful with their actions.

It has been more than an hour since Vince passed. The nurse asks if she can pronounce time of death. I nod my head in acceptance and listen to her say, "Time of death, 5:30 a.m."

Relief and gratitude fill my heart. I squeeze his hand one last time. I am comforted knowing that his journey, our journey, is over. He simply went to sleep. I am grateful for his gentle passing.

I remember the very last words Vince spoke the previous afternoon. "Everything is going as planned." Had he planned to die while Kate was away? We were blessed to have a night nurse with us to watch over him as he passed. I am thankful that I was the last person to speak with him. In the last moments, he felt nothing but absolute love around him and forgiveness.

The nurse phones the funeral home. They will pick up his body for cremation. As we wait, I try to console Vince's mother. She is absolutely grief stricken. She keeps asking why God took him and not her. I hope I never know the pain she must feel, losing a son. I believe the universe has a plan for us all, and Vince's time was done here on earth.

When the funeral home arrives, they recommend the family not be present as they bag the body and remove it. They will exit the house with Vince and not return. I instruct Vince's mother to wait in the guest room in the basement while they take Vince away. Watching his body be removed would be cruel and too difficult.

However, my sense of responsibility for Vince is overpowering. I am waiting in the kitchen area as they bring his body down the stairs closed in a red bag and strapped to a gurney. I open the front door for them, and they slowly roll his body out. I promised Vince he would not be alone at the end so I follow the men to their van. I watch them respectfully load his body in silence. They gently close the doors and turn to nod at me once. With tear-filled eyes, I nod with my acceptance. I step to the back door of the van as the driver climbs in.

I gently place my hand on the window and whisper softly, "I forgive you. Be at peace." The van slowly rolls out of the driveway and down the street. I watch through tears as the van turns the corner.

AN EXCERPT

From *Walking Through the Shadows*

Vince passed a couple of months ago, and the children and I are beginning to adjust to our feelings of loss.

James has settled in at school and is busy finding his way around Cincinnati. He is thriving at college, and while he has moments of sadness, he is focused on his schoolwork.

Kate has completed all her college visits. We have traveled to Los Angeles and Dallas, and she has finalized her school selection. She is in the process of finishing her college applications.

I have returned to work and have begun the process of rebuilding my business. I have also started reconnecting with my friends and neighbors.

More importantly, I have felt a shift in myself emotionally. I am humbled by the experience I shared with Vince. Caring for someone as he or she dies is a very intimate and loving experience. I am grateful that I found forgiveness and that I was able to move beyond our past.

I am proud of the courage I found to care for Vince until the very end. I am pleased that I was able to give Vince the gift of his family. I know he felt comforted being surrounded by the people who loved him the most. I am at peace. I am so proud of James and Kate. We traveled a long road together, and it has made us a stronger family. The tragedy of losing Vince has allowed us to bond in a very special way.

Kate and I enjoy being roommates again. It's just the two of us— except for the myriad of workman who swarm the house painting, refinishing hardwood floors and hanging lights. Kate helped select colors to paint away the sad memories of Vince's illness. She has ordered new furniture and bedding for her room. We are all anxious for a fresh start.

***

Today I receive the lease agreement from Vince's estate. I set it aside with the knowledge that signing the lease is just a formality. Vince has made sure that I can stay in the house as long as I want. All I have to do is pay the utilities and homeowner's association dues every month. This gift provides me with breathing room to support the children for a few more years. I know he loved me as the mother of our children and wanted to make the next few years easier for us.

Later in the day I take a break from the current marketing projects I am working on to read through the lease. My stomach turns upside down, my heart shatters and tears fill my eyes. I can hardly believe what I am reading. Surely there must be a terrible mistake. I continue reviewing the lease only to discover that Vince has instructed the trust that I may live in the home for the next two years and pay the trust rent every month. At the end of two years, the trust will sell the home, and I will need to move.

I am devastated and crushed emotionally. What happened to his promise? Essentially, I must pay James and Kate rent every month to live in their house and take care of them. I feel like such a fool and an idiot. Did my gift of caring for him and giving him the opportunity to spend quality time with his children mean nothing? Did he not understand the sacrifice I made, giving up my life for the last 10 months? I gave him everything I had emotionally and physically. It is almost too horrible to believe.

Fury wells up inside of me. I have worked so hard to forgive all the horrible things he did as a husband and father so we could both have peace. How many times will I have to forgive?

Walking Through the Shadows will be available in 2014. For news and updates, visit www.walkingbeyond.com.

Now available on Amazon: Steps to FORGIVENESS, a guidebook.

A portion of the proceeds from this book will be donated to Houston Methodist Hospital Foundation in support of the Family Resource Center at Houston Methodist Cancer Center.

ADDITIONAL LINKS

Follow Karen on social media:

Twitter: @k_scarpulla

www.facebook.com/karentoddscarpulla

Watch/Listen:

http://www.youtube.com/channel/UCCly-1RPd8xU01rY-eC4lTQ

Download the Meditation App: *Yes You Can Forgive*

iPhone: https://itunes.apple.com/us/app/yes-you-can-forgive/id763798376?ls=1&mt=8

Android: https://play.google.com/store/apps/details?id=com.clearmindsounds.android.yesyoucanforgive

www.ingramcontent.com/pod-product-compliance
Lightning Source LLC
Chambersburg PA
CBHW071001040426
42443CB00007B/600